THE DAILY

THOMAS PAINE

A YEAR OF
COMMON-SENSE

QUOTES

FOR A NONSENSICAL AGE

Edited and with a Foreword by

EDWARD G. GRAY

The University of Chicago Press ✳ Chicago and London

The University of Chicago Press, Chicago 60637
The University of Chicago Press, Ltd., London
© 2020 by The University of Chicago
Published 2020
Printed in the United States of America

29 28 27 26 25 24 23 22 21 20   1 2 3 4 5

ISBN-13: 978-0-226-65351-8 (paper)
ISBN-13: 978-0-226-65365-5 (e-book)
DOI: https://doi.org/10.7208/chicago/9780226653655.001.0001

Library of Congress Cataloging-in-Publication Data
Names: Paine, Thomas, 1737–1809, author. | Gray, Edward G.,
    1964– editor.
Title: The daily Thomas Paine : a year of common-sense
    quotes for a nonsensical age / Thomas Paine, Edward G.
    Gray.
Description: Chicago : University of Chicago Press, 2020. |
    Includes index.
Identifiers: LCCN 2019024292 | ISBN 9780226653518 (paperback)
    | ISBN 9780226653655 (ebook)
Subjects: LCSH: Paine, Thomas, 1737–1809—Quotations.
Classification: LCC JC177 .A5 2020 | DDC 320.01—dc23
LC record available at https://lccn.loc.gov/2019024292

♾ This paper meets the requirements of ANSI/NISO Z39.48-1992
(Permanence of Paper).

THE DAILY THOMAS PAINE

Foreword

We are in a Thomas Paine moment. An unfit executive; law made for lawmakers; a judiciary beholden to political patrons; truculence as foreign policy; cruel income inequality; a constitution on life support; bigoted nationalism masquerading as patriotism.

For the British-born author of *Common Sense*, a 1776 pamphlet that ignited the American Revolution, the origin of all such political dysfunction was clear. It lay in the abuse of power by a crass, self-interested governing elite. Thomas Paine never raised arms against the corrupt leaders he so despised, and he rarely joined the many acts of popular resistance undertaken by those who embraced his writings. But there was no compromise in his methods. Paine believed that his medium, the cheap, widely circulated political pamphlet, would achieve things incremental reform never could. At a time when only the tiniest property-owning minority could vote, structural change would have to come from outside the formal political process. For Paine, it would have to arise from a popular upheaval that transcended national boundaries, that transcended class, and that transcended religious affiliation. The way to ignite such an upheaval was to deploy the most accessible, readily distributed medium of the age.

No one before or since has more masterfully exploited the printed word to disseminate a political message. *Common Sense* and *Rights of Man* (1791–92), Paine's most well-known pamphlets, sold tens of thousands of copies at a time when the typical circulation of such publications rarely reached more than a few thousand. Paine's many enemies, who came to include at least one British prime minister, two American presidents, and assorted reactionaries in Europe and America, struggled in vain to counter his popular reach. Even such gifted polemicists as Edmund Burke, the great parliamentarian and one-time friend of Paine's, came nowhere near matching the scope of Paine's readership.

It was not just the medium that explains Paine's popularity. In communicating his message, Paine deployed the rhetorical arts of London's Grub Street and its public houses. Sarcasm and insult figured in his arsenal as much as his mastery of the ins and outs of eighteenth-century government. As a former agent in the King's Excise Service and as a student of the constitutional underpinnings of Britain's giant fiscal-military state, Paine knew the workings of government as well as any of his contemporaries.

But Paine was no bloviating nob. He wrote for ordinary working people. You will find no arcane classical quotes in his writings and only the most fleeting references to Hobbes, Locke, and other progenitors of his liberal politics. Paine may have understood government as well as any declaiming coffeehouse gentleman, but he had no use for that closed homosocial world and its exclusionary rites. Paine's arguments against monarchy, established religion, and empire, the defining geopolitical institutions of his age, make no reference to cumbersome legal and theological treatises or the many bloated defenses of mercantilism, empire's handmaiden. Paine assumed his audience had no use for such theoretical pomp. Its demand for justice would not be tempered by the ponderous pedantry of the republic of letters.

This is why, in its searing aphoristic clarity, Paine's prose is as striking for its aural effects as it is for its printed bite. And it is why among Paine's fondest admirers are figures whose words most often came to us first as speech. Abraham Lincoln is said to have slept with a copy of Paine's *Rights of Man* by his bed.

We know very little about Paine's writing process, and, from Paine's day to our own, questions have been raised about the authenticity of some of his publications. That the son of a corset maker with little formal schooling could produce such affecting political statements defied credulity and infuriated many of Paine's contemporaries, the learned and lawyerly American revolutionary John Adams notable among them. Paine has also, as he would surely have wanted, defied literary and scholarly categories. Paine is not quite an intellectual, but neither is he the kind of Grub Street hack who cranked out whatever amusements would pay the bills. His prose is supremely artful but rarely poetic. He wrote with an astonishing grasp of contemporary statecraft but never held elected office, and his few forays into government rarely transcended the lowest clerical rungs of the civil service. He was disdainful of books and the learning they contained but routinely enjoyed the company of the greatest minds of his day.

The urgency with which Paine wrote also meant that he rarely stepped back from his public life to reflect on the course of his own career. Unlike practically every one of his famous contemporaries—and there were many of them, from Benjamin Franklin and Thomas Jefferson to the Marquis de Lafayette and George Washington—Paine left only the slightest autobiographical record. If there is one thing that sets Paine apart from these figures, it is that his personal place in history ultimately meant very little to him. What really mattered was justice—justice in the form of transparency in government, justice in the form of fair systems of taxation, justice in the form of welfare for the elderly, the infirm, and children, and for the good and honest men who gave life and limb in the service of national security.

Paine would have failed utterly in our age of media "platform"—a euphemism for vapid marketworthy notoriety. He was as happy antagonizing the prominent and well-placed as he was inciting the anonymous laboring people of the Atlantic world, and he did so in flagrant defiance of the genteel norms of his well-born contemporaries. How glorious and refreshing to contemplate a public figure so hostile to artifice. That Paine's disdain for social convention ultimately left him on the margins of polite society was a fact he came to relish. For it meant that he never compromised his principles for money and fame. But it also meant Paine would die in 1809, destitute and decrepit, the tiny funeral procession which escorted his coffin from New York City to his farm in New Rochelle a bizarre and melancholy last rite for a man whose writings changed the world.

Paine wrote to improve the condition of ordinary people, and his writings were so popular that several of his most famous pamphlets became the most widely read political statements of the age of the American and French Revolutions. But in Paine's case, popularity must not be mistaken for populism. Like the best political essayists, Paine built his assertions on careful argument—argument usually drawing on extensive knowledge of the constitutional foundations of eighteenth-century government. You are as likely to find in Paine's pamphlets lengthy disquisitions about the worldly and very opportunistic origins of absolute monarchy as you are references to the moral philosophy of Jesus and scoffing attacks on privileged, self-serving placeholders. And you will find all of that in plain, unencumbered prose.

What you will not find in Paine's writings are extensive appeals to humanity's basest hatreds. Paine's audience was xenophobic and racist. And periodically in his attacks on Britain and its empire, he echoed their crude hatreds and the accompanying paranoid fantasies. He mentioned Native American frontier brutality and the danger of slave revolts.

But he never attributed these much-feared hazards to race—as many of his readers did. Instead, he saw in them yet more symptoms of the universally corrosive effects of monarchical empire.

Paine was also utterly and openly disdainful of the kind of narrow parochialism that might now appear as ethnic or economic nationalism. He appealed instead to his readers' higher faith in the universality of rights and justice. Anything that obscured the basic goodness of all humans, anything that circumscribed access to a basic sense of well-being, to employment and personal dignity in old age and infirmity, to freedom from tyranny and fear, would be the object of Paine's ire. The territorial claims of nations, the commercial manipulations of empires, the self-serving morality of organized religion, the groundless power of kings and their sycophant courtiers—Paine attacked them all precisely because they inhibited the fundamental human rights to self-definition and self-preservation.

Paine's most controversial pamphlet, *The Age of Reason*, published in 1794, shortly after his arrest and imprisonment in revolutionary Paris, is among the fiercest attacks on organized religion ever written. According to Paine, the clerical establishment, whether the Catholic Church or most of its Protestant descendants, was a vast humbug, perpetrated on naive masses by a cynical clerical elite more interested in their own lavish lifestyle than the well-being of parishioners. Widely admired by Deists in the United States and Britain, the pamphlet would eventually draw the wrath of evangelical Christians who mistook its message for some kind of atheistic screed.

Paine was no atheist. He believed in a benevolent creator, and he believed rational, scientific inquiry was the way to understand that creator's work. Paine was also a revolutionary. He believed that there were times when liberty and justice were more important than order. Much like his friend Thomas Jefferson, he assumed that for all human beings to achieve the rights to which they were naturally and properly entitled, their inherent goodness would have to be tested. The religious and governmental institutions that had so long alienated them from their better natures would have to be torn down and rebuilt, not to serve princes and clerics, but to serve the citizens of the world.

Too often Paine's modern admirers mistake this brand of eighteenth-century liberalism for an anti-statist, market-oriented libertarianism. To be sure, Paine despised the British fiscal-military state. He saw government as an evil, albeit a necessary evil. But when Paine thought of evil government, he thought above all of Britain's government, an entity born of the highest principles but hijacked by special interests, now dependent on the constitutional hoax of hereditary rule and massive state revenues, the latter justified by endless war. The burden of this vast and corrupt system was borne by the ordinary Britons and colonial Americans who paid King George III's tax bills and fought his never-ending wars.

Paine had no problem with taxation in principle. He in fact called on his fellow Americans to pay taxes and, after the American Revolution, wrote in favor of more equitable and progressive tax policy. But he utterly rejected the British government's theft of public monies to support a king and his courtiers. Similarly, Paine delighted in what his near contemporary Adam Smith characterized as a natural human tendency to "truck, barter, and exchange." But for Paine, unlike some of his latter-day disciples, government at its best was more likely to be the servant of commerce than its enemy. In his defense of a national bank and his quest to improve transportation in his adopted home province of Pennsylvania, he championed government-sanctioned public-private partnerships. If subject to appropriate public scrutiny, these partnerships (corporations, in our modern parlance) were agents of good government and public well-being rather than their adversaries. Corporations that detached themselves from the public trust—which in Paine's mind included Britain's East India Company, the Anglican and Catholic churches, and chartered municipalities such as the City of London—earned his wrath. In their ruthless devotion to themselves and their shareholders, they subverted the public good.

Paine was no saint. He drank too much, and his drunken rages often alienated those closest to him. His carbuncled visage, exacerbated by the impurities of eighteenth-century drink, became the Georgian caricaturists' shorthand for crude proletarian demagoguery. Although he demanded justice for the working poor, and although he was among the very first to recognize poverty as an economic rather than a moral problem, his commentary on the plights of women, the enslaved, and non-European victims of European empire is paltry compared to what he wrote about white working men. But, perhaps inevitably, all of those groups would in one way or another eventually call on Paine. Justice demanded it.

Justice also demands that we, too, call on Paine. His words are a tonic for the authoritarianism infecting our politics. They demand from our representatives accountability for fecklessness and for their fealty to public enemies, at home and abroad. They call out a judiciary oblivious to the greater good. And above all they reject the outrageous condescension of a commercialized media, hiding behind a hodge-podge of false equivalencies, innuendo, and the cynical drumbeat of paranoid fantasy.

A Brief Thomas Paine Chronology

THE DAILY THOMAS PAINE

JANUARY

I call not upon a few, but upon all; not on this state, or that state, but on every state. Up and help us. Lay your shoulders to the wheel. Better have too much force than too little, when so great an object is at stake. Let it be told to the future world, that in the depth of winter, when nothing but hope and virtue could survive, that the city and the country, alarmed at one common danger, came forth to meet and to repulse it. Say not that thousands are gone: turn out your tens of thousands: throw not the burden of the day upon providence, but show your faith by your good works, that God may bless you. It matters not where you live, or what rank of life you hold; the evil or the blessing will reach you all. The far and the near, the home counties and the back, the rich and the poor, shall suffer or rejoice alike. The heart that feels not now, is dead.

The American Crisis, Number I (1776)

JANUARY 1

In the following pages I offer nothing more than simple facts, plain arguments, and common sense; and have no other preliminaries to settle with the reader, than that he will divest himself of prejudice and prepossession, and suffer his reason and his feelings to determine for themselves; that he will put *on*, or rather that he will not put *off*, the true character of a man, and generously enlarge his views beyond the present day.

JANUARY 2

Tyranny, like hell, is not easily conquered: yet we have this consolation with us, that the harder the conflict, the more glorious the triumph.

JANUARY 3

Moderation in temper is always a virtue; but moderation in principle is a species of vice.

JANUARY 4
SIX LETTERS TO RHODE ISLAND (1783)

Certainly he, who, not relishing the native liquor of his country, can indulge himself in foreign wines, or can afford to wear the fineries of foreign manufacture, is as proper an object of taxation as he who works a cider-press, or keeps a cow, or tills a few acres of land.

JANUARY 5
TO THE CITIZENS OF THE UNITED STATES (1803)

How nearly is human cunning allied to folly! The animals to whom nature has given the faculty we call *cunning*, know always when to use it, and use it wisely; but when man descends to cunning, he blunders and betrays.

JANUARY 6
RIGHTS OF MAN: PART THE FIRST (1791)

A casual discontinuance of the *practice* of despotism, is not a discontinuance of its *principles*; the former depends on the virtue of the individual who is in immediate possession of the power; the latter, on the virtue and fortitude of the nation.

JANUARY 7
COMMON SENSE (1776)

A long habit of not thinking a thing *wrong*, gives it a superficial appearance of being *right*, and raises at first a formidable outcry in defence of custom. But the tumult soon subsides. Time makes more converts than reason.

JANUARY 8
LETTER TO THE ABBÉ RAYNAL (1782)

The true idea of a great nation, is that which extends and promotes the principles of universal society; whose mind rises above the atmosphere of local thoughts, and considers mankind, of whatever nation or profession they may be, as the work of one Creator.

JANUARY 9
REASONS FOR PRESERVING THE LIFE OF LOUIS CAPET (1793)

The people have beat down royalty, never, never to rise again; they have brought Louis Capet to the bar, and demonstrated in the face of the whole world, the intrigues, the cabals, the falsehood, corruption, and rooted depravity, the inevitable effects of monarchical government. There remains then only one question to be considered, what is to be done with this man?

JANUARY 10
COMMON SENSE (1776)

Though we have been wise enough to shut and lock a door against absolute monarchy, we at the same time have been foolish enough to put the crown in possession of the key.

JANUARY 11
THE AMERICAN CRISIS, NUMBER II (1777)

Universal empire is the prerogative of a writer. His concerns are with all mankind, and though he cannot command their obedience, he can assign them their duty.

JANUARY 12
"TO THE AUTHORS OF *THE REPUBLICAN*" (1791)

The *Hereditary Succession* can never exist as a matter of right; it is a nullity—a *nothing*. To admit the idea is to regard men as a species of property belonging to some individuals, either born or to be born! It is to consider our descendants, and all posterity as mere Animals without a Right or a Will! It is, in fine, the most base, and humiliating idea, that ever degraded the human species, and which, for the honour of Humanity should be destroyed for ever.

JANUARY 13
"ON THE AFFAIRS OF PENNSYLVANIA" (1786)

At the commencement of the revolution, it was supposed that what is called the executive part of a government was the only dangerous part; but we now see that quite as much mischief, if not more, may be done, and as much arbitrary conduct acted, by a legislature.

JANUARY 14
"ATTACK ON PAPER MONEY LAWS" (1786)

The abuse of any power always operates to call the right of that power in question.

JANUARY 15

There is nothing sets the character of a nation in a higher or lower light with others, than the faithfully fulfilling, or perfidiously breaking of treaties.

JANUARY 16

We admit the right of any nation to prohibit the Commerce of another into its own dominions, where there are no treaties to the contrary; but as this right belongs to one side, as well as to the other, there is always a way left to bring avarice and insolence to reason.

JANUARY 17

Those who knew Benjamin Franklin will recollect that his mind was ever young; his temper ever serene. Science, that never grows grey, was always his mistress. He was never without an object; for when we cease to have an object, we become like an invalid in an hospital waiting for death.

JANUARY 18

How trifling, how ridiculous, do the little, paltry cavellings, of a few weak or interested men appear, when weighed against the business of a world.

JANUARY 19

Cultivation is, at least, one of the greatest natural improvements ever made by human invention. It has given to created earth a tenfold value. But the landed monopoly, that began with it, has produced the greatest evil. It has dispossessed more than half the inhabitants of every nation of their natural inheritance, without providing for them, as ought to have been done, as an indemnification for that loss, and has thereby created a species of poverty and wretchedness that did not exist before.

The present state of America is truly alarming to every man who is capable of reflexion. Without law, without government, without any other mode of power than what is founded on, and granted by courtesy. Held together by an unexampled concurrence of sentiment, which is nevertheless subject to change, and which every secret enemy is endeavouring to dissolve. Our present condition, is, Legislation without law; wisdom without a plan; a constitution without a name; and, what is strangely astonishing, perfect Independance contending for Dependance. The instance is without a precedent; the case never existed before; and who can tell what may be the event? The property of no man is secure in the present unbraced system of things. The mind of the multitude is left at random, and seeing no fixed object before them, they pursue such as fancy or opinion starts. Nothing is criminal; there is no such thing as treason; wherefore, every one thinks himself at liberty to act as he pleases.

JANUARY 21

"SHALL LOUIS XVI BE RESPITED?" (1793)

Now, it is an unfortunate circumstance that the individual whose fate we are at present determining has always been regarded by the people of the United States as a friend to their own revolution. Should you come, then, to the resolution of putting Louis to death, you will excite the heartfelt sorrow of your ally. If I were able to speak the French language, I would appear in person at your bar, and, in the name of the American people, ask that Louis be respited.

JANUARY 22
THE FORESTER'S LETTERS (1776)

A treacherous friend in power is the most dangerous of enemies.

JANUARY 23
"THE CRISIS, NUMBER XI" (1782)

We are a young nation just stepping upon the stage of public life, and the eye of the world is upon us to see how we act. We have an enemy that is watching to destroy our reputation, and who will go any length to gain some evidence against us, that may serve to render our conduct suspected and our character odious; because, could she accomplish this, wicked as it is, the world would withdraw from us, as from a people not to be trusted, and our task then would become difficult.

JANUARY 24

RIGHTS OF MAN: PART THE FIRST (1791)

Every thing must have had a beginning, and the fog of time and antiquity should be penetrated to discover it.

JANUARY 25

THE AGE OF REASON: PART THE FIRST (1794)

When we read the obscene stories, the voluptuous debaucheries, the cruel and torturous executions, the unrelenting vindictiveness, with which more than half the Bible is filled, it would be more consistent that we called it the word of a demon, than the word of God. It is a history of wickedness, that has served to corrupt and brutalize mankind; and, for my own part, I sincerely detest it, as I detest every thing that is cruel.

JANUARY 26

"COMMON SENSE, ON FINANCING THE WAR" (1782)

When we think or talk about taxes, we ought to recollect that we lie down in peace, and sleep in safety; that we can follow our farms or stores, or other occupations, in prosperous tranquility; and that these inestimable blessings are procured to us by the taxes that we pay.

JANUARY 27

There is no subject more interesting to every man than the subject of government. His security, be he rich or poor, and, in a great measure, his prosperity, is connected therewith; it is, therefore, his interest, as well as his duty, to make himself acquainted with its principles, and what the practice ought to be.

JANUARY 28

There is in America, more than in any other country, a large body of people who attend quietly to their farms, or follow their several occupations; who pay no regard to the clamors of anonymous scribblers, who think for themselves, and judge of government, not by the fury of newspaper writers, but by the prudent frugality of its measures, and the encouragement it gives to the improvement and prosperity of the country; and who, acting on their own judgment, never come forward in an election but on some important occasion.

JANUARY 29

Of all the innocent passions which actuate the human mind, there is none more universally prevalent than curiosity.

JANUARY 30

The fate of Charles the First, hath only made kings more subtle—not more just.

JANUARY 31

When men, from custom or fashion or any worldly motive, profess or pretend to believe what they do not believe, nor can give any reason for believing, they unship the helm of their morality, and being no longer honest to their own minds they feel no moral difficulty in being unjust to others.

FEBRUARY

From the time I was capable of conceiving an idea, and acting upon it by reflection, I either doubted the truth of the christian system, or thought it to be a strange affair; I scarcely know which it was: but I well remember, when about seven or eight years of age, hearing a sermon read by a relation of mine, who was a great devotee of the church, upon the subject of what is called *Redemption by the Death of the Son of God*. After the sermon was ended I went into the garden, and as I was going down the garden steps (for I perfectly recollect the spot) I revolted at the recollection of what I had heard, and thought to myself that it was making God Almighty act like a passionate man that killed his son when he could not revenge himself any other way; and as I was sure a man would be hanged that did such a thing, I could not see for what purpose they preached such sermons. This was not one of those kind of thoughts that had any thing in it of childish levity; it was to me a serious reflection arising from the idea I had, that God was too good to do such an action, and also too Almighty to be under any necessity of doing it. I believe in the same manner to this moment; and I moreover believe, that any system of religion that has any thing in it that shocks the mind of a child, cannot be a true system.

The Age of Reason: Part the First (1794)

FEBRUARY 1

THE AMERICAN CRISIS, NUMBER I (1776)

These are the times that try men's souls. The summer soldier and the sun-shine patriot will, in this crisis, shrink from the service of his country: but he that stands it *now*, deserves the thanks of man and woman.

FEBRUARY 2

COMMON SENSE (1776)

The king is not to be trusted without being looked after, or in other words, that a thirst for absolute power is the natural disease of monarchy.

FEBRUARY 3

RIGHTS OF MAN: PART THE FIRST (1791)

Every age and generation must be as free to act for itself, *in all cases*, as the ages and generations which preceded it. The vanity and presumption of governing beyond the grave, is the most ridiculous and insolent of all tyrannies.

FEBRUARY 4

"TO SAMUEL ADAMS" (1803)

We can add nothing to eternity.

FEBRUARY 5

TO DANTON (1793)

If every individual is to indulge his private malignancy or his private ambition, to denounce at random and without any kind of proof, all confidence will be undermined and all authority be destroyed.

FEBRUARY 6

THE AGE OF REASON: PART THE FIRST (1794)

I do not believe in the creed professed by the Jewish church, by the Roman church, by the Greek church, by the Turkish church, by the Protestant church, nor by any church that I know of. My own mind is my own church.

FEBRUARY 7

Admitting that Government is a contrivance of human *wisdom*, it must necessarily follow, that hereditary succession, and hereditary rights, (as they are called), can make no part of it, because it is impossible to make wisdom hereditary; and on the other hand, *that* cannot be a wise contrivance, which in its operation may commit the government of a nation to the wisdom of an ideot.

FEBRUARY 8

The world awakens with no pity at your complaints.

FEBRUARY 9

As Europe is our market for trade, we ought to form no partial connection with any part of it.

FEBRUARY 10

It is possible to believe, and I always feel pleasure in encouraging myself to believe it, that there have been men in the world who persuaded themselves that, what is called *a pious fraud*, might, at least under particular circumstances, be productive of some good. But the fraud being once established, could not afterwards be explained; for it is with a pious fraud, as with a bad action, it begets a calamitous necessity of going on.

FEBRUARY 11

"FORGETFULNESS" (1794)

Memory, like a beauty that is always present to hear itself flattered, is flattered by everyone. But the absent and silent goddess, Forgetfulness, has no votaries, and is never thought of; yet we owe her much. She is the goddess of ease, though not of pleasure.

FEBRUARY 12

PROSPECTS ON THE RUBICON (1787)

Right by chance and wrong by system are things so frequently seen in the political world, that it becomes a proof of prudence neither to censure nor applaud too soon.

FEBRUARY 13

LETTER TO THE ABBÉ RAYNAL (1782)

Some passions and vices are but thinly scattered among mankind, and find only here and there a fitness of reception. But prejudice, like the spider, makes every place its home. It has neither taste nor choice of situation, and all that it requires is room. Everywhere, except in fire or water, a spider will live.

FEBRUARY 14

*REASONS FOR PRESERVING THE LIFE
OF LOUIS CAPET* (1793)

Monarchical governments have trained the human race, and inured it to the sanguinary arts and refinements of punishment; and it is exactly the same punishment which has so long shocked the sight and tormented the patience of the people, that now, in their turn, they practise in revenge upon their oppressors. But it becomes us to be strictly on our guard against the abomination and perversity of monarchical examples: as France has been the first of European nations to abolish royalty, let her also be the first to abolish the punishment of death, and to find out a milder and more effectual substitute.

FEBRUARY 15
COMMON SENSE (1776)

As in absolute governments the King is law, so in free countries the law *ought* to be King; and there ought to be no other.

FEBRUARY 16
DISSERTATION ON FIRST PRINCIPLES OF GOVERNMENT (1795)

In a state of nature all men are equal in rights, but they are not equal in power; the weak cannot protect himself against the strong. This being the case, the institution of civil society is for the purpose of making an equalization of powers that shall be parallel to, and a guarantee of the equality of rights.

FEBRUARY 17

LETTER ADDRESSED TO THE ADDRESSERS,
ON THE LATE PROCLAMATION (1792)

It is a dangerous attempt in any Government to say to a Nation, "*thou shalt not read.*"

FEBRUARY 18

RIGHTS OF MAN: PART THE SECOND (1792)

It is painful to see old age working itself to death, in what are called civilized countries, for daily bread.

FEBRUARY 19

THE AGE OF REASON: PART THE FIRST (1794)

Of what use is it, unless it be to teach man something, that his eye is endowed with the power of beholding, to an incomprehensible distance, an immensity of worlds revolving in the ocean of space? Or of what use is it that this immensity of worlds is visible to man? What has man to do with the Pleiades, with Orion, with Sirius, with the star he calls the north star, with the moving orbs he has named Saturn, Jupiter, Mars, Venus, and Mercury, if no uses are to follow from their being visible? A less power of vision would have been sufficient for man, if the immensity he now possesses were given only to waste itself, as it were, on an immense desart of space glittering with shows.

FEBRUARY 20

RIGHTS OF MAN: PART THE SECOND (1792)

Why is it, that scarcely any are executed but the poor?

FEBRUARY 21

THE FORESTER'S LETTERS (1776)

Rousseau proposed a plan for establishing a perpetual European peace; which was, for every state in Europe to send ambassadors to form a General Council, and when any difference happened between any two nations, to refer the matter to arbitration instead of going to arms. This would be forming a kind of European Republic: But the proud and plundering spirit of kings has not peace for its object. They look not at the good of mankind. They set not out upon that plan. And if the history of the creation and the history of kings be compared together the result will be this—that God hath made a world, and kings have robbed him of it.

FEBRUARY 22

COMMON SENSE (1776)

Immediate necessity makes many things convenient, which if continued would grow into oppressions. Expedience and right are different things.

FEBRUARY 23

LETTER TO THE ABBÉ RAYNAL (1782)

Whenever politics are applied to debauch mankind from their integrity, and dissolve the virtue of human nature, they become detestable; and to be a statesman on this plan, is to be a commissioned villain. He who aims at it, leaves a vacancy in his character, which may be filled up with the worst of epithets.

FEBRUARY 24

"ON THE AFFAIRS OF PENNSYLVANIA" (1786)

Public Banks are reckoned among the honors, privileges and advantages of a free people, and are never found among those under a despotic government.

The Almighty lecturer, by displaying the principles of science in the structure of the universe, has invited man to study and to imitation. It is as if he had said to the inhabitants of this globe that we call ours, "I have made an earth for man to dwell upon, and I have rendered the starry heavens visible, to teach him science and the arts. He can now provide for his own comfort, AND LEARN FROM MY MUNIFICENCE TO ALL, TO BE KIND TO EACH OTHER."

Reason and Ignorance, the opposites of each other, influence the great bulk of mankind. If either of these can be rendered sufficiently extensive in a country, the machinery of Government goes easily on. Reason obeys itself; and Ignorance submits to whatever is dictated to it.

Too many nations enslaved the prisoners they took

in war. But to go to nations with whom there is no war, who have no way provoked, without farther design of conquest, purely to catch inoffensive people, like wild beasts, for slaves, is an height of outrage against humanity and justice, that seems left by heathen nations to be practised by pretended Christians. How shameful are all attempts to color and excuse it!

FEBRUARY 28

THE AMERICAN CRISIS, NUMBER V (1778)

To argue with a man who has renounced the use and authority of reason, and whose philosophy consists in holding humanity in contempt, is like administering medicine to the dead, or endeavouring to convert an Atheist by scripture.

FEBRUARY 29

COMMON SENSE (1776)

Wherefore, security being the true design and end of government, it unanswerably follows that whatever *form* thereof appears most likely to ensure it to us, with the least expense and greatest benefit, is preferable to all others.

MARCH

I cannot conceive a greater violation of order, nor a more abominable insult upon morality and upon human understanding, than to see a man sitting in the judgment seat, affecting, by an antiquated foppery of dress, to impress the audience with awe; than causing witnesses and Jury to be sworn to truth and justice, himself having officially sworn the same; then causing to be read a prosecution against a man, charging him with having *wickedly and maliciously written and published a certain false, wicked, and seditious book*; and having gone through all this with a shew of solemnity, as if he saw the eye of the Almighty darting through the roof of the building like a ray of light, turn, in an instant, the whole into a farce, and, in order to obtain a verdict that could not otherwise be obtained, tell the Jury that the charge of *falsely, wickedly, and seditiously*, meant nothing; that *truth* was out of the question; and that whether the person accused spoke truth or falsehood, or intended *virtuously or wickedly*, was the same thing; and finally conclude the wretched inquisitorial scene, by stating some antiquated precedent, equally as abominable as that which is then acting, or giving some opinion of his own, and *falsely called the one and the other—Law.*

Letter Addressed to the Addressers,
on the Late Proclamation (1792)

৩৩ ৩৩

They represent this virtuous and amiable man, Jesus Christ, to be at once both God and man, and also the Son of God, celestially begotten on purpose to be sacrificed, because, they say, that Eve in her longing had eaten an apple.

A despotic government knows no principle but *will*. Whatever the sovereign wills to do, the government admits him the inherent right, and the uncontrolled power of doing. He is restrained by no fixed rule of right and wrong, for he makes the right and wrong himself, and as he pleases. If he happens (for a miracle may happen) to be a man of consummate wisdom, justice and moderation, of a mild affectionate disposition, disposed to business, and understanding and promoting the general good, all the beneficial purposes of government will be answered under his administration, and the people so governed, may, while this is the case, be prosperous and easy.

But as there can be no security that this disposition will last, and this administration continue, and still less security that his successor shall have the same qualities and pursue the same measures; therefore, no people exercising their reason, and understanding their rights, would, of their own choice, invest any one man with such a power.

MARCH 3

RIGHTS OF MAN: PART THE FIRST (1791)

When we survey the wretched condition of man under the monarchical and hereditary systems of Government, dragged from his home by one power, or driven by another, and impoverished by taxes more than by enemies, it becomes evident that those systems are bad, and that a general revolution in the principle and construction of Governments is necessary.

MARCH 4

"THE CRISIS, NUMBER VII" (1778)

My attachment is to all the world and not to any particular part, and if what I advance is right, no matter where or who it comes from.

MARCH 5

Government on the old system, is an assumption of power, for the aggrandisement of itself; on the new, a delegation of power, for the common benefit of society. The former supports itself by keeping up a system of war; the latter promotes a system of peace, as the true means of enriching a nation. The one encourages national prejudices; the other promotes universal society, as the means of universal commerce. The one measures its prosperity, by the quantity of revenue it extorts; the other proves its excellence, by the small quantity of taxes it requires.

MARCH 6
COMMON SENSE (1776)

One of the strongest *natural* proofs of the folly of hereditary right in kings, is, that nature disapproves it, otherwise she would not so frequently turn it into ridicule by giving mankind an *ass for a lion*.

MARCH 7
"THE LAST CRISIS, NUMBER XIII" (1783)

Our union, well and wisely regulated and cemented,

is the cheapest way of being great—the easiest way of being powerful, and the happiest invention in government which the circumstances of America can admit of.

MARCH 8
"THE DREAM INTERPRETED" (1775)

I am apt to think that the wisest men dream the most inconsistently. For as the judgment has nothing or very little to do in regulating the circumstances of a dream, it necessarily follows that the more powerful and creative the imagination is, the wilder it runs in that state of unrestrained invention; while those who are unable to wander out of the track of common thinking when awake, never exceed the boundaries of common nature when asleep.

MARCH 9
RIGHTS OF MAN: PART THE FIRST (1791)

If the present generation, or any other, are disposed to be slaves, it does not lessen the right of the succeeding generation to be free: wrongs cannot have a legal descent.

But how will the persons who have been induced to read the *Rights of Man*, by the clamour that has been raised against it, be surprized to find, that, instead of a wicked, inflamatory work, instead of a licencious and profligate performance, it abounds with principles of government that are uncontrovertible—with arguments which every reader will feel, are unanswerable—with plans for the increase of commerce and manufactures—for the extinction of war—for the education of the children of the poor—for the comfortable support of the aged and decayed persons of both sexes—for the relief of the army and navy, and, in short, for the promotion of every thing that can benefit the moral, civil and political condition of Man.

MARCH 11

RIGHTS OF MAN: PART THE SECOND (1792)

Scarcely any thing presents a more degrading character of national greatness, than its being thrown into confusion by any thing happening to, or acted by, an individual; and the ridiculousness of the scene is often increased by the natural insignificance of the person by whom it is occasioned.

MARCH 12

If we take a survey of ages and of countries, we shall find the women, almost—without exception—at all times and in all places, adored and oppressed. Man, who has never neglected an opportunity of exerting his power, in paying homage to their beauty, has always availed himself of their weakness. He has been at once their tyrant and their slave.

MARCH 13

Every generation is equal in rights to the generations which preceded it, by the same rule that every individual is born equal in rights with his contemporary.

MARCH 14

Were it possible that the Congress of America, could be so lost to their duty, and to the interest of their constituents, as to offer General Washington, as president of America, a million a year, he would not, and he could not, accept it. His sense of honour is of another kind.

MARCH 15

COMMON SENSE (1776)

No man was a warmer wisher for reconciliation than
myself, before the fatal nineteenth of April 1775, but
the moment the event of that day was made known,
I rejected the hardened, sullen tempered Pharoah of
England for ever; and disdain the wretch, that with
the pretended title of FATHER OF HIS PEOPLE can
unfeelingly hear of their slaughter, and composedly
sleep with their blood upon his soul.

MARCH 16

RIGHTS OF MAN: PART THE SECOND (1792)

In the present state of things, a labouring man, with
a wife and two or three children, does not pay less
than between seven and eight pounds a year in taxes.
He is not sensible of this, because it is disguised to
him in the articles which he buys, and he thinks only
of their dearness; but as the taxes take from him,
at least, a fourth part of his yearly earnings, he is
consequently disabled from providing for a family,
especially, if himself, or any of them, are afflicted
with sickness.

MARCH 17

I should not be a whit the more able to write a book, because my name were altered; neither would any man, now called a King or a Lord, have a whit the more sense than he now has, were he to call himself Thomas Paine.

MARCH 18

Government by Monks, who know nothing of the world beyond the walls of a Convent, is as consistent as government by Kings.

MARCH 19

By being our own masters, independent of any foreign one, we have Europe for our friends, and the prospect of an endless peace among ourselves.

MARCH 20

When it shall be said in any country in the world, my poor are happy; neither ignorance nor distress is to be found among them; my jails are empty of prisoners, my streets of beggars; the aged are not in want, the taxes are not oppressive; the rational world is my friend, because I am the friend of its happiness: when these things can be said, then may that country boast its constitution and its government.

MARCH 21

"AN ESSAY FOR THE USE OF NEW REPUBLICANS IN THEIR OPPOSITION TO MONARCHY" (1792)

Royalty and Popery have had the same goal to attain and have been supported by the same deceptions; they are now falling into the same decay under the rays of the same Light.

MARCH 22

COMMON SENSE (1776)

Mankind being originally equals in the order of creation, the equality could only be destroyed by some subsequent circumstance; the distinctions of rich, and poor, may in a great measure be accounted for, and that without having recourse to the harsh, ill-sounding names of oppression and avarice. Oppression is often the *consequence*, but seldom or never the *means* of riches; and though avarice will preserve a man from being necessitously poor, it generally makes him too timorous to be wealthy.

MARCH 23

"THE NECESSITY OF TAXATION" (1782)

Never let it be said, that the country who could do what America has done, defrauded the widow and the orphan of their property, and the soldier of his pay.

MARCH 24

THE AGE OF REASON: PART THE FIRST (1794)

Latter times have laid all the blame upon the Goths and Vandals, but, however unwilling the partizans of the Christian system may be to believe or to acknowledge it, it is nevertheless true, that the age of ignorance commenced with the Christian system. There was more knowledge in the world before that period than for many centuries afterwards; and as to religious knowledge, the christian system, as already said, was only another species of mythology; and the mythology to which it succeeded, was a corruption of an ancient system of theism.

MARCH 25

RIGHTS OF MAN: PART THE FIRST (1791)

It is over the lowest class of mankind that government by terror is intended to operate, and it is on them that it operates to the worst effect. They have sense enough to feel they are the objects aimed at; and they inflict in their turn the examples of terror they have been instructed to practise.

MARCH 26

THE AGE OF REASON: PART THE FIRST (1794)

You will do me the justice to remember, that I have always strenuously supported the Right of every Man to his own opinion, however different that opinion might be to mine. He who denies to another this right, makes a slave of himself to his present opinion, because he precludes himself the right of changing it.

MARCH 27
COMMON SENSE (1776)

Of more worth is one honest man to society, and in the sight of God, than all the crowned ruffians that ever lived.

MARCH 28
RIGHTS OF MAN: PART THE SECOND (1792)

What is called the splendor of a throne is no other than the corruption of the state. It is made up of a band of parasites, living in luxurious indolence, out of the public taxes.

MARCH 29
"TO SAMUEL ADAMS" (1803)

The case, my friend, is that the world has been overrun with fable and creeds of human invention, with sectaries of whole nations against all other nations, and sectaries of those sectaries in each of them against each other. Every sectary, except the Quakers, has been a persecutor. Those who fled from persecution persecuted in their turn, and it is this confusion of creeds that has filled the world with persecution and deluged it with blood.

MARCH 30

Men who look upon themselves born to reign, and others to obey, soon grow insolent; selected from the rest of mankind their minds are early poisoned by importance; and the world they act in differs so materially from the world at large, that they have but little opportunity of knowing its true interests, and when they succeed to the government are frequently the most ignorant and unfit of any throughout the dominions.

MARCH 31

RIGHTS OF MAN: PART THE FIRST (1791)

He pities the plumage, but forgets the dying bird.

APRIL

We have heard the *Rights of Man* called a *levelling* system; but the only system to which the word *levelling* is truly applicable, is the hereditary monarchical system. It is a system of *mental levelling*. It indiscriminately admits every species of character to the same authority. Vice and virtue, ignorance and wisdom, in short, every quality, good or bad, is put on the same level. Kings succeed each other, not as rationals, but as animals. It signifies not what their mental or moral characters are. Can we then be surprised at the abject state of the human mind in monarchical countries, when the government itself is formed on such an abject levelling system?—It has no fixed character. To day it is one thing; to-morrow it is something else. It changes with the temper of every succeeding individual, and is subject to all the varieties of each. It is government through the medium of passions and accidents. It appears under all the various characters of childhood, decrepitude, dotage, a thing at nurse, in leading-strings, or in crutches. It reverses the wholesome order of nature. It occasionally puts children over men, and the conceits of non-age over wisdom and experience. In short, we cannot conceive a more ridiculous figure of government, than hereditary succession, in all its cases, presents.

Rights of Man: Part the Second (1792)

APRIL 1

It is impossible to calculate the moral mischief, if I may so express it, that mental lying has produced in society. When a man has so far corrupted and prostituted the chastity of his mind, as to subscribe his professional belief to things he does not believe, he has prepared himself for the commission of every other crime.

APRIL 2

Where knowledge is a duty, ignorance is a crime.

APRIL 3

Death is not the monarch of the dead, but of the dying. The moment he obtains a conquest he loses a subject, and, like the foolish King you serve, will, in the end, war himself out of all dominion.

APRIL 4

RIGHTS OF MAN: PART THE SECOND (1792)

Mankind are not now to be told they shall not think, or they shall not read; and publications that go no farther than to investigate principles of government, to invite men to reason and to reflect, and to shew the errors and excellences of different systems, have a right to appear.

APRIL 5

THE AGE OF REASON: PART THE FIRST (1794)

It is only by the exercise of reason, that man can discover God. Take away that reason, and he would be incapable of understanding any thing; and, in this case, it would be just as consistent to read even the book called the Bible, to a horse as to a man.

APRIL 6

RIGHTS OF MAN: PART THE SECOND (1792)

Independence is my happiness, and I view things as they are, without regard to place or person; my country is the world, and my religion is to do good.

APRIL 7

Letters, the tongue of the world, have in some measure brought all mankind acquainted, and by an extension of their uses are every day promoting some new friendship. Through them distant nations became capable of conversation, and losing by degrees the awkwardness of strangers, and the moroseness of suspicion, they learn to know and understand each other. Science, the partisan of no country, but the beneficent patroness of all, has liberally opened a temple where all may meet. Her influence on the mind, like the sun on the chilled earth, has long been preparing it for higher cultivation and further improvement. The philosopher of one country sees not an enemy in the philosopher of another: he takes his seat in the temple of science, and asks not who sits beside him.

APRIL 8

COMMON SENSE (1776)

Society in every state is a blessing, but government even in its best state is but a necessary evil.

APRIL 9

If those who vote the supplies are the same persons who receive the supplies when voted, and are to account for the expenditure of those supplies to those who voted them, it is *themselves accountable to themselves*, and the Comedy of Errors concludes with the Pantomine of HUSH.

APRIL 10

That there are men in all countries to whom a state of war is a mine of wealth, is a fact never to be doubted. Characters like these naturally breed in the putrefaction of distempered times, and after fattening on the disease they perish with it, or impregnated with the stench retreat into obscurity.

APRIL 11

That which is now called natural philosophy, embracing the whole circle of science, of which astronomy occupies the chief place, is the study of the works of God and of the power and wisdom of God in his works, and is the true theology.

APRIL 12

I am not induced by motives of pride, party, or resentment to espouse the doctrine of separation and independance; I am clearly, positively, and conscientiously persuaded that it is the true interest of this continent to be so; that every thing short of *that* is mere patchwork, that it can afford no lasting felicity,—that it is leaving the sword to our children, and shrinking back at a time, when, a little more, a little farther, would have rendered this continent the glory of the earth.

APRIL 13

For the domestic happiness of Britain and the peace of the world I wish she had not a foot of land but what is circumscribed within her own island. Extent of dominion hath been her ruin, and instead of civilizing others hath brutalized herself.

APRIL 14

RIGHTS OF MAN: PART THE SECOND (1792)

No one man is capable, without the aid of society, of supplying his own wants.

APRIL 15

COMMON SENSE (1776)

This new world hath been the asylum for the persecuted lovers of civil and religious liberty from *every part* of Europe. Hither have they fled, not from the tender embraces of the mother, but from the cruelty of the monster; and it is so far true of England, that the same tyranny which drove the first emigrants from home, pursues their descendants still.

APRIL 16

The apology that is sometimes made for continuing to teach the dead languages is, that they are taught at a time when a child is not capable of exerting any other mental faculty than that of memory. But this is altogether erroneous. The human mind has a natural disposition to scientific knowledge, and to the things connected with it. The first and favourite amusement of a child, even before it begins to play, is that of imitating the works of man. It builds houses with cards or sticks; it navigates the little ocean of a bowl of water with a paper boat; or dams the stream of a gutter, and contrives something which it calls a mill; and it interests itself in the fate of its works with a care that resembles affection. It afterwards goes to school, where its genius is killed by the barren study of a dead language, and the philosopher is lost in the linguist.

APRIL 17

Government does not consist in a contrast between prisons and palaces, between poverty and pomp; it is not instituted to rob the needy of his mite, and increase the wretchedness of the wretched.

APRIL 18

COMMON SENSE (1776)

In page 33, I threw out a few thoughts on the propriety of a Continental Charter, (for I only presume to offer hints, not plans) and in this place, I take the liberty of rementioning the subject, by observing, that a charter is to be understood as a bond of solemn obligation, which the whole enters into, to support the right of every separate part, whether of religion, personal freedom, or property. A firm bargain and a right reckoning make long friends.

APRIL 19

RIGHTS OF MAN: PART THE FIRST (1791)

The French constitution says, That the right of war and peace is in the nation. Where else should it reside, but in those who are to pay the expence?

APRIL 20

COMMON SENSE (1776)

And when a man seriously reflects on the idolatrous homage which is paid to the persons of Kings, he need not wonder, that the Almighty, ever jealous of his honor, should disapprove of a form of government which so impiously invades the prerogative of heaven.

THE AGE OF REASON: PART THE FIRST (1794)

The Christian mythologists, after having confined Satan in a pit, were obliged to let him out again, to bring on the sequel of the fable. He is then introduced into the garden of Eden in the shape of a snake, or a serpent, and in that shape he enters into familiar conversation with Eve, who is no ways surprised to hear a snake talk; and the issue of this tête-à-tête is, that he persuades her to eat an apple, and the eating of that apple, damns all mankind.

APRIL 22

"THE NECESSITY OF TAXATION" (1782)

Government and the people do not in America constitute distinct bodies. They are one, and their interest the same.

APRIL 23

RIGHTS OF MAN: PART THE SECOND (1792)

What is called a *republic*, is not any *particular form* of government. It is wholly characteristical of the pur-port, matter, or object for which government ought to be instituted, and on which it is to be employed, RES-PUBLICA, the public affairs, or the public good; or, literally translated, the *public thing*.

APRIL 24
"AFRICAN SLAVERY IN AMERICA" (1775)

How just, how suitable to our crime is the punish-ment with which providence threatens us? We have enslaved multitudes, and shed much innocent blood in doing it; and now are threatened with the same. And while others evils are confessed, and bewailed, why not this especially, and publicly; than which no other vice, if all others, has brought so much guilt on the land?

APRIL 25
RIGHTS OF MAN: PART THE FIRST (1791)

That *civil government* is necessary, all civilized nations will agree; but civil government is republi-can government.

APRIL 26

A long succession of insolent severity, and the separation finally occasioned by the commencement of hostilities at Lexington, on the nineteenth of April, 1775, naturally produced a new disposition of thinking. As the mind closed itself toward England, it opened itself toward the world, and our prejudices like our oppressions, underwent, though less observed, a mental examination; until we found the former as inconsistent with reason and benevolence, as the latter were repugnant to our civil and political rights.

APRIL 27

Surely she loves to fish in troubled waters, and drink the cup of contention, or she would not now think of mingling her affairs with those of America. It would be like a foolish dotard taking to his arms the bride that despises him, or who has placed on his head the ensigns of her disgust. It is kissing the hand that boxes his ears, and proposing to renew the exchange. The thought is as servile as the war was wicked, and shews the last scene of the drama as inconsistent as the first.

Governments now act as if they were afraid to awaken a single reflection in man. They are softly leading him to the sepulchre of precedents, to deaden his faculties and call his attention from the scene of revolutions. They feel that he is arriving at knowledge faster than they wish, and their policy of precedents is the barometer of their fears. This political popery, like the ecclesiastical popery of old, has had its day, and is hastening to its exit. The ragged relic and the antiquated precedent, the monk and the monarch, will moulder together.

APRIL 29

COMMON SENSE (1776)

No nation ought to be without a debt. A national debt is a national bond.

APRIL 30

THE AGE OF REASON: PART THE FIRST (1794)

As to the christian system of faith, it appears to me as a species of atheism; a sort of religious denial of God. It professes to believe in a man rather than in

God. It is a compound made up chiefly of manism with but little deism, and is as near to atheism as twilight is to darkness. It introduces between man and his maker an opaque body which it calls a redeemer; as the moon introduces her opaque self between the earth and the sun, and it produces by this means a religious or an irreligious eclipse of light. It has put the whole orb of reason into shade.

MAY

It has been thought a considerable advance towards establishing the principles of Freedom, to say, that government is a compact between those who govern and those who are governed: but this cannot be true, because it is putting the effect before the cause; for as man must have existed before governments existed, there necessarily was a time when governments did not exist, and consequently there could originally exist no governors to form such a compact with. The fact therefore must be, that the *individuals themselves*, each in his own personal and sovereign right, *entered into a compact with each other* to produce a government: and this is the only mode in which governments have a right to arise, and the only principle on which they have a right to exist.

Rights of Man: Part the First (1791)

MAY 1

Common sense will tell us, that the power which hath endeavoured to subdue us, is of all others the most improper to defend us.

MAY 2

RIGHTS OF MAN: PART THE FIRST (1791)

Lay then the axe to the root, and teach governments humanity. It is their sanguinary punishments which corrupt mankind. In England, the punishment in certain cases, is by *hanging drawing*, and *quartering*; the heart of the sufferer is cut out, and held up to the view of the populace. In France, under the former government, the punishments were not less barbarous. Who does not remember the execution of Damien, torn to pieces by horses? The effect of those cruel spectacles exhibited to the populace, is to destroy tenderness, or excite revenge; and by the base and false idea of governing men by terror, instead of reason, they become precedents.

MAY 3

Accustom a people to believe that priests or any other class of men can forgive sins, and you will have sins in abundance.

MAY 4

But you are probably buoyed up by a set of wretched mortals, who, having deceived themselves, are cringing with the duplicity of a spaniel for a little temporary bread. Those men will tell you just what you please. It is their interest to amuse in order to lengthen out their protection. They study to keep you amongst them for that very purpose; and in proportion as you disregard their advice and grow callous to their complaints, they will stretch into improbability, and pepper off their flattery the higher. Characters like these are to be found in every country, and every country will despise them.

MAY 5

RIGHTS OF MAN: PART THE SECOND (1792)

All hereditary government is in its nature tyranny.

MAY 6

DISSERTATIONS ON GOVERNMENT (1786)

One of the evils of paper money is, that it turns the whole country into stock jobbers. The precariousness of its value and the uncertainty of its fate continually operate, night and day, to produce this destructive effect. Having no real value in itself it depends for support upon accident, caprice and party, and as it is the interest of some to depreciate and of others to raise its value, there is a continual invention going on that destroys the morals of the country.

MAY 7

COMMON SENSE (1776)

From Britain we can expect nothing but ruin. If she is once admitted to the government of America again, this Continent will not be worth living in. Jealousies will be always arising, insurrections will be constantly happening; and who will go forth to quell them? Who will venture his life to reduce his own countrymen to a foreign obedience? The difference between Pennsylvania and Connecticut, respecting some unlocated lands, shews the insignificance of a British government, and fully proves, that nothing but Continental authority can regulate Continental matters.

MAY 8

"TO THE AUTHORS OF *THE REPUBLICAN*" (1791)

It is perhaps impossible in the first steps which are made in a Revolution, to avoid all kind of error, in Principle or in Practice, or in some instances to prevent the Combination of both. Before the sense of a Nation is sufficiently enlightened, and before Men have entered into the habits of a free Communication with each other of their natural thoughts, a certain reserve—a timid prudence seizes on the human Mind, and prevents it from attaining its level, with that vigour and promptitude which belongs to *Right*.—An Example of this influence discovers itself in the commencement of the present Revolution.

MAY 9

THE FORESTER'S LETTERS (1776)

It is the duty of the public, at this time, to scrutinize closely into the conduct of their Committee Members, Members of Assembly, and Delegates in Congress; to know what they do, and their motives for so doing. Without doing this, we shall never know who to confide in; but shall constantly mistake friends for enemies, and enemies for friends, till in this confusion of persons we sacrifice the cause.

MAY 10

THE AGE OF REASON: PART THE FIRST (1794)

All national institutions of churches, whether Jewish, Christian, or Turkish, appear to me no other than human inventions set up to terrify and enslave mankind, and monopolize power and profit.

MAY 11

WORSHIP AND CHURCH BELLS:
A LETTER TO CAMILLE JORDAN (1797)

The seeds of good principles, and the literary means of advancement in the world, are laid in early life. Instead, therefore, of consuming the substance of the nation upon priests, whose life at best is a life of idleness, let us think of providing for the education of those who have not the means of doing it themselves.

MAY 12

So monstrous is the making and keeping them slaves at all, abstracted from the barbarous usage they suffer, and the many evils attending the practice; as selling husbands away from wives, children from parents, and from each other, in violation of sacred and natural ties; and opening the way for adulteries, incests, and many shocking consequences, for all of which the guilty masters must answer to the final Judge.

MAY 13

RIGHTS OF MAN: PART THE FIRST (1791)

The original hereditary despotism resident in the person of the King, divides and subdivides itself into a thousand shapes and forms, till at last the whole of it is acted by deputation. This was the case in France; and against this species of despotism, proceeding on through an endless labyrinth of office till the source of it is scarcely perceptible, there is no mode of redress. It strengthens itself by assuming the appearance of duty, and tyrannises under the pretence of obeying.

MAY 14

It is at all times necessary, and more particularly so during the progress of a revolution, and until right ideas confirm themselves by habit, that we frequently refresh our patriotism by reference to first principles. It is by tracing things to their origin, that we learn to understand them; and it is by keeping that line and that origin always in view, that we never forget them.

MAY 15

Whatever the form or constitution of government may be, it ought to have no other object than the *general* happiness. When, instead of this, it operates to create and encrease wretchedness in any of the parts of society, it is on a wrong system, and reformation is necessary.

MAY 16

A government of our own is our natural right: And when a man seriously reflects on the precariousness of human affairs, he will become convinced, that it is infinitely wiser and safer, to form a constitution of our own in a cool deliberate manner, while we have it in our power, than to trust such an interesting event to time and chance.

MAY 17

THE AMERICAN CRISIS, NUMBER V (1778)

There is not in the compass of language a sufficiency of words to express the baseness of your King, his Ministry and his Army. They have refined upon villainy till it wants a name. To the fiercer vices of former ages they have added the dregs and scummings of the most finished rascality, and are so completely sunk in serpentine deceit, that there is not left among them *one* generous enemy.

MAY 18

LETTER ADDRESSED TO THE ADDRESSERS,
ON THE LATE PROCLAMATION (1792)

That there are two distinct classes of men in the nation, those who pay taxes, and those who receive and live upon the taxes, is evident at first sight; and when taxation is carried to excess, it cannot fail to disunite those two, and something of this kind is now beginning to appear.

MAY 19

Separate an individual from society, and give him an island or a continent to possess, and he cannot acquire personal property. He cannot become rich. So inseparably are the means connected with the end, in all cases, that where the former do not exist, the latter cannot be obtained. All accumulation, therefore, of personal property, beyond what a man's own hands produce, is derived to him by living in society; and he owes, on every principle of justice, of gratitude, and of civilization, a part of that accumulation back again to society from whence the whole came.

MAY 20

Every generation is, and must be, competent to all the purposes which its occasions require. It is the living, and not the dead, that are to be accommodated. When man ceases to be, his power and his wants cease with him; and having no longer any participation in the concerns of this world, he has no longer any authority in directing who shall be its governors, or how its government shall be organized, or how administered.

I look through the present trouble to a time of tranquillity, when we shall have it in our power to set an example of peace to all the world.

If, to expose the fraud and imposition of monarchy, and every species of hereditary government—to lessen the oppression of taxes—to propose plans for the education of helpless infancy, and the comfortable support of the aged and distressed—to endeavour to conciliate nations to each other—to extirpate the horrid practice of war—to promote universal peace, civilization, and commerce—and to break the chains of political superstition, and raise degraded man to his proper rank;—if these things be libellous, let me live the life of a Libeller, and let the name of LIBELLER be engraven on my tomb.

MAY 23

RIGHTS OF MAN: PART THE SECOND (1792)

Its first settlers were emigrants from different European nations, and of diversified professions of religion, retiring from the governmental persecutions of the old world, and meeting in the new, not as enemies, but as brothers.

MAY 24

"COMMON SENSE, ON FINANCING THE WAR" (1782)

In America almost every farmer lives on his own lands, and in England not one in a hundred does.

MAY 25

RIGHTS OF MAN: PART THE SECOND (1792)

It is not for the benefit of those who exercise the powers of government, that constitutions, and the governments issuing from them, are established.

MAY 26
COMMON SENSE (1776)

In point of right and good order, there is something very ridiculous, that a youth of twenty-one (which hath often happened) shall say to several millions of people, older and wiser than himself, I forbid this or that act of yours to be law.

MAY 27
THE AMERICAN CRISIS, NUMBER III (1777)

War and desolation are become the trades of the old world; and America neither could, nor can be under the government of Britain without becoming a sharer of her guilt, and a partner in all the dismal commerce of death. The spirit of duelling, extended on a national scale, is a proper character for European wars. They have seldom any other motive than pride, or any other object than fame. The conquerors and the conquered are generally ruined alike, and the chief difference at last is, that the one marches home with his honours, and the other without them.

Government is nothing more than a national association; and the object of this association is the good of all, as well individually as collectively.

As the exercise of Government requires talents and abilities, and as talents and abilities cannot have hereditary descent, it is evident that hereditary succession requires a belief from man, to which his reason cannot subscribe, and which can only be established upon his ignorance; and the more ignorant any country is, the better it is fitted for this species of Government.

How easy is it to abuse truth and language, when men, by habitual wickedness, have learned to set justice at defiance.

The sole reason why Royalty, with all its visionary splendor, its assumed necessity, the superstitious idolatry that follows in its train, was created was for the purpose of exacting from its victims excessive taxation and willing submission.

JUNE

It is the good fortune of many to live distant from the scene of sorrow; the evil is not sufficiently brought to *their* doors to make *them* feel the precariousness with which all American property is possessed. But let our imaginations transport us for a few moments to Boston, that seat of wretchedness will teach us wisdom, and instruct us for ever to renounce a power in whom we can have no trust. The inhabitants of that unfortunate city, who but a few months ago were in ease and affluence, have now no other alternative than to stay and starve, or turn out to beg. Endangered by the fire of their friends if they continue within the city, and plundered by the soldiery if they leave it. In their present condition they are prisoners without the hope of redemption, and in a general attack for their relief, they would be exposed to the fury of both armies.

Common Sense (1776)

JUNE 1

THE AGE OF REASON: PART THE FIRST (1794)

The event that served more than any other, to break the first link in this long chain of despotic ignorance, is that known by the name of the reformation by Luther. From that time, though it does not appear to have made any part of the intention of Luther, or of those who are called reformers, the Sciences began to revive, and Liberality, their natural associate, began to appear. This was the only public good the reformation did; for with respect to religious good, it might as well not have taken place. The mythology still continued the same; and a multiplicity of national popes grew out of the downfall of the Pope of Christendom.

JUNE 2

COMMON SENSE (1776)

The King and his worthless adherents are got at their old game of dividing the Continent, and there are not wanting among us, Printers, who will be busy in spreading specious falsehoods.

JUNE 3

A government on the principles on which constitutional governments arising out of society are established, cannot have the right of altering itself.

JUNE 4

Notwithstanding the mystery with which the science of government has been enveloped, for the purpose of enslaving, plundering, and imposing upon mankind, it is of all things the least mysterious, and the most easy to be understood.

JUNE 5

As the present generation of people in England did not make the Government, they are not accountable for any of its defects; but that sooner or later it must come into their hands to undergo a constitutional reformation, is as certain as that the same thing has happened in France.

It is surprising that an authority which can be supported with so much ease, and so little expence, and capable of such extensive advantages to the country, should be cavelled at by those whose duty it is to watch over it, and whose existance, as a people depends upon it. But this, perhaps, will ever be the case, till some misfortune awaken us into reason, and the instance now before us is but a gentle beginning of what America must expect, unless she guards her Union with nicer care and stricter honour. United, she is formidable, and that with the least possible charge, a Nation can be so: Separated, she is a medley of individual nothings, subject to the sport of foreign Nations.

JUNE 7

RIGHTS OF MAN: PART THE FIRST (1791)

With respect to what are called denominations of religion, if every one is left to judge of its own religion, there is no such thing as a religion that is wrong; but if they are to judge of each others religion, there is no such thing as a religion that is right; and therefore, all the world is right, or all the world is wrong.

Let them call me rebel, and welcome; I feel no concern from it; but I should suffer the misery of devils, were I to make a whore of my soul, by swearing allegiance to one whose character is that of a sottish, stupid, stubborn, worthless, brutish man.

The *Honorable* plunderer of his country, or the *Right Honorable* murderer of mankind, create such a contrast of ideas as exhibit a monster rather than a man. Virtue is inflamed at the violation, and sober reason calls it nonsense.

Immortal power is not a human right.

JUNE 11
PROSPECTS ON THE RUBICON (1787)

War involves in its progress such a train of unfore-seen and unsupposed circumstances, such a com-bination of foreign matters, that no human wisdom can calculate the end. It has but one thing certain, and that is increase of TAXES.

JUNE 12
THE AGE OF REASON: PART THE SECOND (1795)

The mere man of pleasure is miserable in old age, and the mere drudge in business is but little bet-ter: whereas natural philosophy, mathematical, and mechanical science, are a continual source of tran-quil pleasure; and in spite of the gloomy dogma of priests and of superstition, the study of those things is the study of the true theology. It teaches man to know and to admire the Creator, for the principles of science are in the creation, and are unchangeable, and of divine origin.

JUNE 13
THE FORESTER'S LETTERS (1776)

Painful as the task of speaking truth must some-times be, yet I cannot avoid giving the following hint, because much, nay almost everything depends upon it; and that is, *a thorough knowledge of the persons whom we trust.*

JUNE 14

RIGHTS OF MAN: PART THE SECOND (1792)

So deeply rooted were all the governments of the old world, and so effectually had the tyranny and the antiquity of habit established itself over the mind, that no beginning could be made in Asia, Africa, or Europe, to reform the political condition of man. Freedom had been hunted round the globe; reason was considered as rebellion; and the slavery of fear had made men afraid to think.

JUNE 15

"THE LAST CRISIS, NUMBER XIII" (1783)

Rome, once the proud mistress of the universe, was originally a band of ruffians. Plunder and rapine made her rich, and her oppression of millions made her great.

JUNE 16

The independence of America, considered merely as a separation from England, would have been a matter but of little importance, had it not been accompanied by a revolution in the principles and practice of governments.

JUNE 17

To talk of friendship with those in whom our reason forbids us to have faith, and our affections wounded through a thousand pores instruct us to detest, is madness and folly.

JUNE 18

The revolutions that have taken place in other European countries, have been excited by personal hatred. The rage was against the man, and he became the victim. But, in the instance of France, we see a revolution generated in the rational contemplation of the rights of man, and distinguishing from the beginning between persons and principles.

JUNE 19

TO BENJAMIN RUSH (1790)

I despair of seeing an Abolition of the infernal trafic in Negroes—we must push that matter further on your side the water—I wish that a few well instructed Negroes could be sent among their Brethren in Bondage, for until they are enabled to take their own part nothing will be done.

JUNE 20

*LETTER ADDRESSED TO THE ADDRESSERS,
ON THE LATE PROCLAMATION (1792)*

Of what use in the science and system of Government is what is called a Lord Chamberlain, a Master and a Mistress of the Robes, a Master of the Horse, a Master of the Hawks, and an hundred other such things. Laws derive no additional force, nor additional excellence, from such mummery.

JUNE 21

RIGHTS OF MAN: PART THE SECOND (1792)

If there is a country in the world, where concord, according to common calculation, would be least expected, it is America. Made up, as it is, of people from different nations, accustomed to different forms and habits of government, speaking different languages, and more different in their modes of worship, it would appear that the union of such a people was impracticable; but by the simple operation of constructing government on the principles of society and the rights of man, every difficulty retires, and all the parts are brought into cordial unison.

JUNE 22

TO DANTON (1793)

Calumny is a species of treachery that ought to be punished as well as any other kind of treachery. It is a private vice productive of public evils; because it is possible to irritate men into disaffection by continual calumny who never intended to be disaffected.

JUNE 23

COMMON SENSE (1776)

Perhaps the disorders which threatened, or seemed to threaten on the decease of a leader and the choice of a new one (for elections among ruffians could not be very orderly) induced many at first to favor hereditary pretensions; by which means it happened, as it hath happened since, that what at first was submit-

ted to as a convenience, was afterwards claimed as
a right.

JUNE 24

THE AGE OF REASON: PART THE FIRST (1794)

Moral principle speaks universally for itself.

JUNE 25

RIGHTS OF MAN: PART THE SECOND (1792)

It could have been no difficult thing in the early and
solitary ages of the world, while the chief employment of men was that of attending flocks and herds,
for a banditti of ruffians to overrun a country, and
lay it under contributions. Their power being thus
established, the chief of the band contrived to lose
the name of Robber in that of Monarch; and hence
the origin of Monarchy and Kings.

JUNE 26

"THE NECESSITY OF TAXATION" (1782)

In vain are all our huzzas for liberty, without accompanying them with solid support. They will neither
fill the soldier's belly, nor cloathe his back, they will

neither pay the public creditors, nor purchase our supplies. They are well enough in their places, and though they are the effusion of our hearts, they are no part of our substance.

JUNE 27

COMMON SENSE (1776)

I have heard it asserted by some, that as America hath flourished under her former connexion with Great-Britain, that the same connexion is necessary towards her future-happiness, and will always have the same effect. Nothing can be more fallacious than this kind of argument. We may as well assert, that because a child has thrived upon milk, that it is never to have meat; or that the first twenty years of our lives is to become a precedent for the next twenty. But even this is admitting more than is true, for I answer roundly, that America would have flourished as much, and probably much more, had no European power had any thing to do with her. The commerce by which she hath enriched herself are the necessaries of life, and will always have a market while eating is the custom of Europe.

JUNE 28

When an author undertakes to treat of public happiness he ought to be certain that he does not mistake passion for right, nor imagination for principle. Principle, like truth, needs no contrivance. It will ever tell its own tale, and tell it the same way. But where this is not the case, every page must be watched, recollected, and compared like an invented story.

JUNE 29

The government of a free country, properly speaking, is not in the persons, but in the laws.

JUNE 30

The idea, always dangerous to society as it is derogatory to the Almighty, that priests could forgive sins, though it seemed to exist no longer, had blunted the feelings of humanity, and callously prepared men for the commission of all crimes. The intolerant spirit of church persecution had transferred itself into politics; the tribunals, stiled revolutionary, supplied the place of an inquisition, and the guillotine of the stake. I saw many of my most intimate friends destroyed; others daily carried to prison; and I had reason to believe, and had also intimations given me, that the same danger was approaching myself.

JULY

It was my fate to come to America a few months before the breaking out of hostilities. I found the disposition of the people such, that they might have been led by a thread and governed by a reed. Their suspicion was quick and penetrating, but their attachment to Britain was obstinate, and it was, at that time, a kind of treason to speak against it. They disliked the Ministry, but they esteemed the nation. Their ideas of grievance operated without resentment, and their single object was reconciliation. Bad as I believed the Ministry to be, I never conceived them capable of a measure so rash and wicked as the commencing of hostilities; much less did I imagine the nation would encourage it. I viewed the dispute as a kind of law-suit, in which I supposed the parties would find a way either to decide or settle it. I had no thoughts of independence or of arms. The world could not then have persuaded me that I should be either a soldier or an author. If I had any talents for either they were buried in me, and might ever have continued so, had not the necessity of the times dragged and driven them into action. I had formed my plan of life, and conceiving myself happy, wished every body else so. But when the country, into which

I had but just put my foot, was set on fire about my ears it was time to stir. It was time for every man to stir. Those who had been long settled had something to defend; those who were just come had something to pursue; and the call and the concern was equal and universal.

"The Crisis, Number VII" (1778)

JULY 1

What we obtain too cheap, we esteem too lightly: 'tis dearness only that gives every thing its value. Heaven knows how to set a proper price upon its goods; and it would be strange, indeed, if so celestial an article as freedom should not be highly rated. Britain, with an army to enforce her tyranny, has declared that she has a right, not only to tax, but "to bind us in all cases whatsoever:" and if being bound in that manner is not slavery, there is not such a thing as slavery upon earth. Even the expression is impious: for so unlimited a power can belong only to God.

JULY 2

Nonsense ought to be treated as nonsense wherever it be found; and had this been done in the rational manner it ought to be done, instead of intimating and mincing the matter, as has been too much the case, the nonsense and false doctrine of the Bible, with all the aid that priestcraft can give, could never have stood their ground against the divine reason that God has given to man.

JULY 3

DISSERTATIONS ON GOVERNMENT (1786)

In republics, such as those established in America, the sovereign power, or the power over which there is no control, and which controls all others, remains where nature placed it—in the people; for the people in America are the fountain of power.

JULY 4

COMMON SENSE (1776)

The cause of America is in a great measure the cause of all mankind.

JULY 5

RIGHTS OF MAN: PART THE FIRST (1791)

The heads stuck upon spikes, which remained for years upon Temple-bar, differed nothing in the horror of the scene from those carried about upon spikes at Paris: yet this was done by the English government. It may perhaps be said, that it signifies nothing to a man what is done to him after he is dead; but it signifies much to the living: it either tortures their feelings, or hardens their hearts; and in either case, it instructs them how to punish when power falls into their hands.

JULY 6

I am not one of those who are fond of believing there is much of that which is called wilful lying, or lying originally, except in the case of men setting up to be prophets, as in the old testament, for prophesying is lying professionally. In almost all other cases it is not difficult to discover the progress by which even simple supposition with the aid of credulity will in time grow into a lye, and at last be told as a fact: and whenever we can find a charitable reason for a thing of this kind we ought not to indulge a severe one.

JULY 7

Despotic government supports itself by abject civilization, in which debasement of the human mind, and wretchedness in the mass of the people, are the chief criterians. Such governments consider man merely as an animal; that the exercise of intellectual faculty is not his privilege; *that he has nothing to do with the laws, but to obey them*; and they politically depend more upon breaking the spirit of the people by poverty, than they fear enraging it by desperation.

JULY 8

Where there are no distinctions there can be no supe-
riority, perfect equality affords no temptation. The
republics of Europe are all (and we may say always)
in peace. Holland and Swisserland are without wars,
foreign or domestic: Monarchical governments, it
is true, are never long at rest; the crown itself is a
temptation to enterprizing ruffians at *home*; and that
degree of pride and insolence ever attendant on regal
authority, swells into a rupture with foreign powers, in instances, where a republican government,
by being formed on more natural principles, would
negociate the mistake.

JULY 9

Government founded on a *moral theory, on a system of universal peace, on the indefeasible hereditary
Rights of Man*, is now revolving from west to east, by a
stronger impulse than the government of the sword
revolved from east to west.

JULY 10

Character is much easier kept than recovered, and that man, if any such there be, who, from sinister views, or littleness of soul, lends unseen his hand to injure it, contrives a wound it will never be in his power to heal.

JULY 11

DISSERTATION ON FIRST PRINCIPLES OF GOVERNMENT (1795)

The moral principle of revolutions is to instruct, not to destroy.

JULY 12

THE AGE OF REASON: PART THE FIRST (1794)

Nothing that is here said can apply, even with the most distant disrespect, to the *real* character of Jesus Christ. He was a virtuous and an amiable man. The morality that he preached and practised was of the most benevolent kind; and though similar systems of morality had been preached by Confucius, and by some of the Greek philosophers, many years before; by the quakers since; and by many good men in all ages; it has not been exceeded by any.

JULY 13

A nation under a well regulated government, should permit none to remain uninstructed. It is monarchical and aristocratical government only that requires ignorance for its support.

JULY 14

The sun never shined on a cause of greater worth. 'Tis not the affair of a city, a county, a province, or a kingdom, but of a continent—of at least one eighth part of the habitable globe. 'Tis not the concern of a day, a year, or an age; posterity are virtually involved in the contest, and will be more or less affected, even to the end of time, by the proceedings now. Now is the seed time of continental union, faith and honor. The least fracture now will be like a name engraved with the point of a pin on the tender rind of a young oak; the wound will enlarge with the tree, and posterity read it in full grown characters.

JULY 15

To see it in our power to make a world happy—to teach mankind the art of being so—to exhibit, on the theatre of the universe a character hitherto unknown—and to have, as it were, a new creation intrusted to our hands, are honors that command reflection, and can neither be too highly estimated, nor too gratefully received.

JULY 16

REASONS FOR PRESERVING THE LIFE OF LOUIS CAPET (1793)

France is not satisfied with exposing the guilt of the monarch. She has penetrated into the vices and horrors of the monarchy. She has shown them clear as daylight, and forever crushed that system; and he, whoever he may be, that should ever dare to reclaim those rights would be regarded not as a pretender, but punished as a traitor.

JULY 17

RIGHTS OF MAN: PART THE SECOND (1792)

If men will permit themselves to think, as rational

beings ought to think, nothing can appear more ridiculous and absurd, exclusive of all moral reflections, than to be at the expence of building navies, filling them with men, and then hauling them into the ocean, to try which can sink each other fastest. Peace, which costs nothing, is attended with infinitely more advantage, than any victory with all its expence. But this, though it best answers the purpose of nations, does not that of court governments, whose habited policy is pretence for taxation, places, and offices.

JULY 18

"COMMON SENSE, ON FINANCING THE WAR" (1782)

How is the army to bear the want of food, cloathing and other necessaries? The man who is at home can turn himself a thousand ways, and find as many means of ease, convenience or relief: But a soldier's life admits of none of those: Their wants cannot be supplied from themselves: For an army, though it is the defence of a State, is at the same time the child of a country, and must be provided for in every thing.

JULY 19

PUBLIC GOOD (1780)

A right, to be truly so, must be right within itself:

yet many things have obtained the name of rights, which are originally founded in wrong. Of this kind are all rights by mere conquest, power or violence.

In the cool moments of reflection we are obliged to allow that the mode by which such a right is obtained is not the best suited to that spirit of universal justice which ought to preside equally over all mankind.

JULY 20

RIGHTS OF MAN: PART THE SECOND (1792)

There can be no such thing as a nation flourishing alone in commerce; she can only participate; and the destruction of it in any part must necessarily affect all.

JULY 21

"EMANCIPATION OF SLAVES" (1780)

We find in the distribution of the human species, that the most fertile as well as the most barren parts of the earth are inhabited by men of complexions different from ours, and from each other; from whence we may reasonably as well as religiously infer, that He, who placed them in their various situations, has extended equally His care and protection to all, and that it becomes not us to counteract His mercies.

JULY 22

Things, like men, are seldom understood rightly at first sight.

JULY 23

A republican government hath more *true grandeur* in it than a kingly one. On the part of the public it is more consistent with freemen to appoint their rulers than to have them born; and on the part of those who preside, it is far nobler to be a ruler by the choice of the people, than a king by the chance of birth.

JULY 24

I saw, during the American Revolution, the exceeding inconvenience that arose by having the government of Congress within the limits of any municipal jurisdiction. Congress first resided in Philadelphia, and after a residence of four years it found it necessary to leave it. It then adjourned to the state of Jersey. It afterwards removed to New York; it again removed from New York to Philadelphia, and after experiencing in every one of these places the great inconvenience of a government, it formed the project of building a town, not within the limits of any municipal jurisdiction, for the future residence of Congress. In any one of the places where Congress resided, the municipal authority privately or openly opposed itself to the authority of Congress, and the people of each of these places expected more attention from Congress than their equal share with the other States amounted to. The same thing now takes place in France, but in a far greater excess.

JULY 25
"THE CRISIS, NUMBER VIII" (1780)

It was not Newton's honor, neither could it be his pride, that he was an Englishman, but that he was a philosopher: The Heavens had liberated him from the prejudices of an island, and science had expanded his soul as boundless as his studies.

JULY 26
RIGHTS OF MAN: PART THE SECOND (1792)

The evils of the aristocratical system are so great and numerous, so inconsistent with every thing that is just, wise, natural, and beneficent, that when they are considered, there ought not to be a doubt that many, who are now classed under that description, will wish to see such a system abolished.

JULY 27

COMMON SENSE (1776)

Sincerely wishing, that as men and christians, ye may always fully and uninterruptedly enjoy every civil and religious right; and be, in your turn, the means of securing it to others; but that the example which ye have unwisely set, of mingling religion with politics, *may be disavowed and reprobated by every inhabitant* of AMERICA.

JULY 28

RIGHTS OF MAN: PART THE FIRST (1791)

Titles are but nick-names, and every nick-name is a title. The thing is perfectly harmless in itself; but it marks a sort of foppery in the human character, which degrades it.

JULY 29

The first aristocrats in all countries were brigands.
Those of latter times, sycophants.

JULY 30

Perhaps no man bred up in the stile of an absolute
King, ever possessed a heart so little disposed to the
exercise of that species of power as the present King
of France. But the principles of the government itself
still remained the same. The Monarch and the Monarchy were distinct and separate things; and it was
against the established despotism of the latter, and
not against the person or principles of the former,
that the revolt commenced, and the revolution has
been carried.

JULY 31

The most detestable wickedness, the most horrid cruelties, and the greatest miseries that have
afflicted the human race, have had their origin in
this thing called revelation or revealed religion.

AUGUST

I had seen enough of the miseries of war, to wish it might never more have existence in the world, and that some other mode might be found out to settle the differences that should occasionally arise in the neighbourhood of nations. This certainly might be done if Courts were disposed to set honestly about it, or if countries were enlightened enough not to be made the dupes of Courts. The people of America had been bred up in the same prejudices against France, which at that time characterized the people of England; but experience and an acquaintance with the French Nation have most effectually shown to the Americans the falsehood of those prejudices; and I do not believe that a more cordial and confidential intercourse exists between any two countries than between America and France.

Rights of Man: Part the First (1791)

AUGUST 1

COMMON SENSE (1776)

Some writers have so confounded society with government, as to leave little or no distinction between them; whereas they are not only different, but have different origins. Society is produced by our wants, and government by our wickedness; the former promotes our happiness *positively* by uniting our affections, the latter *negatively* by restraining our vices. The one encourages intercourse, the other creates distinctions. The first is a patron, the last a punisher.

AUGUST 2

THE AGE OF REASON: PART THE FIRST (1794)

Infidelity does not consist in believing, or in disbelieving: it consists in professing to believe what he does not believe.

AUGUST 3

"THE CRISIS, NUMBER VI" (1778)

We have a perfect idea of a *natural* enemy when we think of the *Devil*, because the enmity is perpetual, unalterable and unabateable. It admits of neither peace, truce or treaty; consequently the warfare is eternal, and therefore it is natural. But man with man cannot arrange in the same opposition. Their quarrels are accidental and equivocally created. They become friends or enemies as the change of temper or the cast of interest inclines them. The Creator of man did not constitute him the natural enemy of each other. He has not made any one order of beings so. Even wolves may quarrel, still they herd together. If any two nations are so, then must all nations be so, otherwise it is not nature but custom, and the offence frequently originates with the accuser.

AUGUST 4

"A REPUBLICAN MANIFESTO" (1791)

An office that may be filled by a person without talent or experience, an office that does not require virtue or wisdom, for its due exercise, an office which is the reward of birth, and which may consequently devolve on a madman, an imbecile or a tyrant, is, in the very nature of things, an absurdity, and, whatever its ostentation, has no real utility.

AUGUST 5

RIGHTS OF MAN: PART THE SECOND (1792)

The present age will hereafter merit to be called

the Age of reason, and the present generation will appear to the future as the Adam of a new world.

AUGUST 6

LETTER ADDRESSED TO THE ADDRESSERS, ON THE LATE PROCLAMATION (1792)

The right of altering any part of a Government cannot, as already observed, reside in the Government, or that Government might make itself what it pleased.

AUGUST 7

RIGHTS OF MAN: PART THE SECOND (1792)

That which is called government, or rather that which we ought to conceive government to be, is no more than some common center, in which all the parts of society unite.

AUGUST 8

COMMON SENSE (1776)

America doth not yet know what opulence is, and although the progress which she hath made stands unparalleled in the history of other nations, it is but childhood, compared with what she would be capable of arriving at, had she, as she ought to have, the legislative powers in her own hands.

AUGUST 9

RIGHTS OF MAN: PART THE FIRST (1791)

If there existed a man so transcendantly wise above all others, that his wisdom was necessary to instruct a nation, some reason might be offered for monarchy; but when we cast our eyes about a country, and observe how every part understands its own affairs; and when we look around the world, and see that of all men in it, the race of kings are the most insignificant in capacity, our reason cannot fail to ask us—What are those men kept for?

AUGUST 10

DISSERTATION ON FIRST PRINCIPLES OF GOVERNMENT (1795)

Had a constitution been established two years ago (as ought to have been done) the violences that have since desolated France, and injured the character of the revolution, would, in my opinion, have been prevented. The nation would then have been a bond of union, and every individual would have known the line of conduct he was to follow. But, instead of this, a revolutionary government, a thing without either principle or authority, was substituted in its place; virtue and crime depended upon accident; and that which was patriotism one day, became treason the next. All these things have followed from the want of a constitution.

AUGUST 11

RIGHTS OF MAN: PART THE SECOND (1792)

With respect to another class of men, the inferior clergy, I forbear to enlarge on their condition; but all partialities and prejudices for, or against, different modes and forms of religion aside, common justice will determine, whether there ought to be an income of twenty or thirty pounds a year to one man, and of ten thousand to another. I speak on this subject with the more freedom, because I am known not to be a Presbyterian; and therefore the cant cry of court sycophants, about church and meeting, kept up to amuse and bewilder the nation, cannot be raised against me.

AUGUST 12

Calumny becomes harmless and defeats itself when it attempts to act upon too large a scale.

AUGUST 13

RIGHTS OF MAN: PART THE FIRST (1791)

The constitution of a country is not the act of its government, but of the people constituting a government. It is the body of elements, to which you can refer, and quote article by article; and which contains the principles on which the government shall be established, the manner in which it shall be organized, the powers it shall have, the mode of elections, the duration of parliaments, or by what other name such bodies may be called; the powers which the executive part of the government shall have; and, in fine, every thing that relates to the compleat organization of a civil government, and the principles on which it shall act, and by which it shall be bound.

AUGUST 14

THE AMERICAN CRISIS, NUMBER II (1777)

All countries have sooner or later been called to their

reckoning; the proudest empires have sunk when the balance was struck; and Britain, like an individual penitent, must undergo her day of sorrow, and the sooner it happens to her the better.

AUGUST 15

In my publications, I follow the rule I began with in "Common Sense," that is, to consult nobody, nor to let anybody see what I write till it appears publicly. Were I to do otherwise the case would be that between the timidity of some, who are so afraid of doing wrong that they never do right, the puny judgment of others, and the despicable craft of preferring *expedient to right*, as if the world was a world of babies in leading strings, I should get forward with nothing.

AUGUST 16

WORSHIP AND CHURCH BELLS:
A LETTER TO CAMILLE JORDAN (1797)

No man ought to make a living by religion.

AUGUST 17

With what kind of parental reflections can the father or mother contemplate their younger offspring. By nature they are children, and by marriage they are heirs; but by aristocracy they are bastards and orphans.

AUGUST 18

I draw my idea of the form of government from a principle in nature, which no art can overturn, viz. that the more simple any thing is, the less liable it is to be disordered, and the easier repaired when disordered; and with this maxim in view, I offer a few remarks on the so much boasted constitution of England. That it was noble for the dark and slavish times in which it was erected is granted. When the world was over-run with tyranny the least remove therefrom was a glorious rescue. But that it is imperfect, subject to convulsions, and incapable of producing what it seems to promise, is easily demonstrated.

It is easy to conceive, that a band of interested men, such as Placemen, Pensioners, Lords of the bed-chamber, Lords of the kitchen, Lords of the necessary-house, and the Lord knows what besides, can find as many reasons for monarchy as their salaries, paid at the expence of the country, amount to; but if I ask the farmer, the manufacturer, the merchant, the tradesman and down through all the occupations of life to the common labourer, what service monarchy is to him? he can give me no answer.

An avidity to punish is always dangerous to liberty. It leads men to stretch, to misinterpret, and to misapply even the best of laws. He that would make his own liberty secure, must guard even his enemy from oppression; for if he violates this duty, he establishes a precedent that will reach to himself.

The most extraordinary of all things called miracles, related in the New Testament, is that of the devil flying away with Jesus Christ, and carrying him to the top of a high mountain; and to the top of the highest pinacle of the temple, and showing him, and promising to him *all the kingdoms of the world*. How happened it that he did not discover America? or is it only with *kingdoms* that his sooty highness has any interest?

The Spanish proverb says, "*there never was a cover large enough to hide itself.*"

That some desperate wretches should be willing to steal and enslave men by violence and murder for gain, is rather lamentable than strange. But that many civilized, nay, Christianized people should approve, and be concerned in the savage practice, is surprising; and still persist, though it has been so often proved contrary to the light of nature, to every principle of justice and humanity, and even good policy, by a succession of eminent men, and several late publications.

AUGUST 24

"A REPUBLICAN MANIFESTO" (1791)

The greatness of a people is not, as monarchs claim, based on the magnificence of a king, but in the people's sense of its own dignity and on its contempt for the brutal follies and crimes which have, under the leadership of kings, desolated the whole of Europe.

AUGUST 25

RIGHTS OF MAN: PART THE FIRST (1791)

All religions are in their nature kind and benign, and united with principles of morality. They could not have made proselites at first, by professing any thing that was vicious, cruel, persecuting, or immoral. Like every thing else, they had their beginning; and they proceeded by persuasion, exhortation, and example. How then is it that they lose their native mildness, and become morose and intolerant?

AUGUST 26

If the judgment sleeps while the imagination keeps awake, the dream will be a riotous assemblage of misshapen images and ranting ideas, and the more active the imagination is the wilder the dream will be. The most inconsistent and the most impossible things will appear right; because that faculty whose province it is to keep order is in a state of absence. The master of the school is gone out and the boys are in an uproar.

AUGUST 27

COMMON SENSE (1776)

A government which cannot preserve the peace, is no government at all.

AUGUST 28

"TO THE EARL OF SHELBURNE" (1782)

The British army in America care not how long the war lasts. They enjoy an easy and indolent life. They fatten on the folly of one country and the spoils of another; and, between their plunder and their pay, may go home rich. But the case is very different with the labouring farmer, the working tradesman, and the necessitous poor in England, the sweat of whose brow goes day after day to feed, in prodigality and sloth, the army that is robbing both them and us. Removed from the eye of the country that supports them, and distant from the government that employs them, they cut and carve for themselves and there is none to call them to account.

AUGUST 29

"TO SAMUEL ADAMS" (1803)

A man does not serve God when he prays, for it is himself he is trying to serve; and as to hiring or paying men to pray, as if the Deity needed instruction, it is, in my opinion, an abomination.

AUGUST 30

RIGHTS OF MAN: PART THE SECOND (1792)

The man who is in the receipt of a million a year is the last person to promote a spirit of reform, lest, in the event, it should reach to himself.

COMMON SENSE (1776)

O ye that love mankind! Ye that dare oppose, not only the tyranny, but the tyrant, stand forth! Every spot of the old world is over-run with oppression. Freedom hath been hunted round the globe. Asia, and Africa, have long expelled her.—Europe regards her like a stranger, and England hath given her warning to depart. O! receive the fugitive, and prepare in time an asylum for mankind.

SEPTEMBER

Youth is the seed time of good habits, as well in nations as in individuals. It might be difficult, if not impossible, to form the Continent into one government half a century hence. The vast variety of interests, occasioned by an increase of trade and population, would create confusion. Colony would be against colony. Each being able might scorn each other's assistance: and while the proud and foolish gloried in their little distinctions, the wise would lament that the union had not been formed before. Wherefore, the *present time* is the *true time* for establishing it. The intimacy which is contracted in infancy, and the friendship which is formed in misfortune, are, of all others, the most lasting and unalterable. Our present union is marked with both these characters: we are young, and we have been distressed; but our concord hath withstood our troubles, and fixes a memorable æra for posterity to glory in.

The present time, likewise, is that peculiar time, which never happens to a nation but once, *viz.* the time of forming itself into a government. Most nations have let slip the opportunity, and by that means have been compelled to receive laws from their conquerors, instead of making laws for themselves. First, they had a king, and then a form of government; whereas, the articles or charter of government, should be formed first, and men delegated to execute them afterward: but from the errors of other nations, let us learn wisdom, and lay hold of the present opportunity—*To begin government at the right end*.

Common Sense (1776)

SEPTEMBER 1

RIGHTS OF MAN: PART THE FIRST (1791)

That there are men in all countries who get their living by war, and by keeping up the quarrels of Nations, is as shocking as it is true; but when those who are concerned in the government of a country, make it their study to sow discord, and cultivate prejudices between Nations, it becomes the more unpardonable.

SEPTEMBER 2

CASE OF THE OFFICERS OF EXCISE (1772)

There is a striking difference between dishonesty arising from want of food, and want of principle. The first is worthy of compassion, the other of punishment.

SEPTEMBER 3

THE AGE OF REASON: PART THE FIRST (1794)

But how was Jesus Christ to make any thing known to all nations? He could speak but one language, which was Hebrew; and there are in the world several hundred languages. Scarcely any two nations speak the same language, or understand each other; and as to translations, every man who knows any thing of languages, knows that it is impossible to translate from one language into another not only without losing a great part of the original, but frequently of mistaking the sense: and besides all this, the art of printing was wholly unknown at the time Christ lived.

SEPTEMBER 4

"THE NECESSITY OF TAXATION" (1782)

It is pity but some other word beside taxation had been devised for so noble and extraordinary an occasion, as the protection of liberty and the establishment of an independant world.

SEPTEMBER 5

RIGHTS OF MAN: PART THE FIRST (1791)

Ignorance is of a peculiar nature: once dispelled, and it is impossible to re-establish it. It is not originally a thing of itself, but is only the absence of knowledge; and though man may be *kept* ignorant, he cannot be *made* ignorant. The mind, in discovering truth, acts in the same manner as it acts through the eye in discovering objects; when once any object has been seen, it is impossible to put the mind back to the same condition it was in before it saw it.

SEPTEMBER 6

TO DANTON (1793)

When I left America in the year 1787, it was my intention to return the year following, but the French Revolution, and the prospect it afforded of extending the principles of liberty and fraternity through the greater part of Europe, have induced me to prolong my stay upwards of six years. I now despair of seeing the great object of European liberty accomplished, and my despair arises not from the combined foreign powers, not from the intrigues of aristocracy and priestcraft, but from the tumultuous misconduct with which the internal affairs of the present Revolution are conducted.

SEPTEMBER 7

RIGHTS OF MAN: PART THE SECOND (1792)

It would be an act of despotism, or what in England is called arbitrary power, to make a law to prohibit investigating the principles, good or bad, on which such a law, or any other is founded.

SEPTEMBER 8

RIGHTS OF MAN: PART THE SECOND (1792)

If universal peace, civilization, and commerce, are ever to be the happy lot of man, it cannot be accomplished but by a revolution in the system of governments.

SEPTEMBER 9

LETTER ADDRESSED TO THE ADDRESSERS,
ON THE LATE PROCLAMATION (1792)

It is error only, and not truth, that shrinks from enquiry.

SEPTEMBER 10

RIGHTS OF MAN: PART THE SECOND (1792)

In all my publications, where the matter would admit, I have been an advocate for commerce, because I am a friend to its effects. It is a pacific system, operating to cordialize mankind, by rendering nations, as well as individuals, useful to each other.

SEPTEMBER 11

As in my political works my motive and object have been to give man an elevated sense of his own character, and free him from the slavish and superstitious absurdity of monarchy and hereditary government, so in my publications on religious subjects my endeavors have been directed to bring man to a right use of the reason that God has given him, to impress on him the great principles of divine morality, justice, mercy and a benevolent disposition to all men and to all creatures, and to inspire in him a spirit of trust, confidence and consolation in his Creator, unshackled by the fables of books pretending to be *the Word of God*.

SEPTEMBER 12

A nation is not a body, the figure of which is to be represented by the human body; but is like a body contained within a circle, having a common center, in which every radius meets; and that center is formed by representation.

It was the cause of America that made me an author. The force with which it struck my mind, and the dangerous condition the country appeared to me in, by courting an impossible and an unnatural reconciliation with those who were determined to reduce her, instead of striking out into the only line that could cement and save her, A DECLARATION OF INDEPENDENCE, made it impossible for me, feeling as I did, to be silent: and if, in the course of more than seven years, I have rendered her any service, I have likewise added something to the reputation of literature, by freely and disinterestedly employing it in the great cause of mankind, and showing that there may be genius without prostitution.

The true, and only true basis of representative government is equality of rights. Every man has a right to one vote, and no more, in the choice of representatives. The rich have no more right to exclude the poor from the right of voting, or of electing and being elected, than the poor have to exclude the rich; and wherever it is attempted, or proposed, on either side, it is a question of force, and not of right.

SEPTEMBER 15

RIGHTS OF MAN: PART THE FIRST (1791)

Nothing can be more terrible to a Court or a Courtier, than the Revolution of France. That which is a blessing to Nations, is bitterness to them; and as their existence depends on the duplicity of a country, they tremble at the approach of principles, and dread the precedent that threatens their overthrow.

SEPTEMBER 16

LETTER ADDRESSED TO THE ADDRESSERS,
ON THE LATE PROCLAMATION (1792)

When the rich plunder the poor of his rights, it becomes an example to the poor to plunder the rich of his property; for the rights of the one are as much property to him as wealth is property to the other, and the *little all* is as dear as the *much*. It is only by setting out on just principles that men are trained to be just to each other; and it will always be found, that when the rich protect the rights of the poor, the poor will protect the property of the rich.

SEPTEMBER 17

RIGHTS OF MAN: PART THE SECOND (1792)

Government ought to be as much open to improvement as any thing which appertains to man, instead of which it has been monopolized from age to age, by the most ignorant and vicious of the human race. Need we any other proof of their wretched management, than the excess of debts and taxes with which every nation groans, and the quarrels into which they have precipitated the world?

SEPTEMBER 18

THE AMERICAN CRISIS, NUMBER II (1777)

There are such things as national sins, and though the punishment of individuals may be reserved to *another* world, national punishment can only be inflicted in *this* world.

SEPTEMBER 19

COMMON SENSE (1776)

Suspicion is the companion of mean souls, and the bane of all good society.

SEPTEMBER 20

RIGHTS OF MAN: PART THE FIRST (1791)

The patriots of France have discovered in good time, that rank and dignity in society must take a new ground. The old one has fallen through.—It must now take the substantial ground of character, instead of the chimerical ground of titles; and they have brought their titles to the altar, and made of them a burnt-offering to Reason.

SEPTEMBER 21

RIGHTS OF MAN: PART THE SECOND (1792)

Government is not a trade which any man or body of men has a right to set up and exercise for his own emolument, but is altogether a trust, in right of those by whom that trust is delegated, and by whom it is always resumeable. It has of itself no rights; they are altogether duties.

SEPTEMBER 22

"THE CRISIS, NUMBER VIII" (1780)

Fire, sword and want, as far as the arms of Britain could extend them, have been spread with wanton cruelty along the coast of America; and while you, remote from the scene of suffering, had nothing to lose and as little to dread, the information reached you like a tale of antiquity, in which the distance of time defaces the conception, and changes the severest sorrows into conversable amusement.

SEPTEMBER 23

RIGHTS OF MAN: PART THE FIRST (1791)

If I ask a man in America, if he wants a King? he retorts, and asks me if I take him for an ideot?

SEPTEMBER 24

DISSERTATIONS ON GOVERNMENT (1786)

When a people agree to form themselves into a republic (for the word *republic* means the *public good*, or the good of the whole, in contra-distinction to the despotic form, which makes the good of the sovereign, or of one man, the only object of the government), when I say, they agree to do this, it is to be understood that they mutually resolve and pledge themselves to each other, rich and poor alike, to support and maintain this rule of equal justice among them. They therefore renounce not only the despotic form, but despotic principle, as well of governing as of being governed by mere will and power, and substitute in its place a government of justice.

From whence then could arise the solitary and strange conceit that the Almighty, who had millions of worlds equally dependent on his protection, should quit the care of all the rest, and come to die in our world, because, they say, one man and one woman had eaten an apple. And, on the other hand, are we to suppose that every world, in the boundless creation, had an Eve, an apple, a serpent, and a redeemer. In this case, the person who is irreverently called the Son of God, and sometimes God himself, would have nothing else to do than to travel from world to world, in an endless succession of death, with scarcely a momentary interval of life.

It is not because a part of the government is elective, that makes it less, a despotism, if the persons so elected, possess afterwards, as a parliament, unlimited powers. Election, in this case, becomes separated from representation, and the candidates are candidates for despotism.

SEPTEMBER 27

AGRARIAN JUSTICE (1797)

The superstitious awe, the enslaving reverence, that formerly surrounded affluence, is passing away in all countries, and leaving the possessor of property to the convulsion of accidents. When wealth and splendour, instead of fascinating the multitude, excite emotions of disgust; when, instead of drawing forth admiration, it is beheld as an insult upon wretchedness; when the ostentatious appearance it makes, serves to call the right of it in question, the case of property becomes critical, and it is only in a system of justice that the possessor can contemplate security.

SEPTEMBER 28

RIGHTS OF MAN: PART THE FIRST (1791)

Who, then, art thou, vain dust and ashes! by whatever name thou art called, whether a King, a Bishop, a Church or a State, a Parliament, or any thing else, that obtrudest thine insignificance between the soul of man and its Maker? Mind thine own concerns. If he believes not as thou believest, it is a proof that thou believest not as he believeth, and there is no earthly power can determine between you.

SEPTEMBER 29

"THE CRISIS, NUMBER IX" (1780)

At a Crisis, big, like the present, with expectation and events, the whole country is called to unanimity and exertion. Not an ability ought now to sleep that can produce but a mite to the general good, nor even a whisper suffered to pass that militates against it. The necessity of the case, and the importance of the consequences, admit no delay from a friend, no apology from an enemy. To spare now, would be the height of extravagance, and to consult present ease, would sacrifice it, perhaps, for ever.

SEPTEMBER 30

LETTER TO THE ABBÉ RAYNAL (1782)

Of more use was *one* philosopher, though a heathen, to the world, than all the heathen conquerors that ever existed.

OCTOBER

To see women and children wandering in the severity of winter with the broken remains of a well furnished house, and seeking shelter in every crib and hut, were matters you had no conception of. You knew not what it was to stand by and see your goods chopt up for fuel, and your beds ript to pieces to make packages for plunder. The misery of others, like a tempestuous night, added to the pleasures of your own security. You even enjoyed the storm, by contemplating the difference of conditions; and that which carried sorrow into the breasts of thousands, served but to heighten in you a species of tranquil pride. Yet these are but the fainter sufferings of war, when compared with carnage and slaughter, the miseries of a military hospital, or a town in flames.

"The Crisis, Number VIII" (1780)

OCTOBER 1

There is something exceedingly ridiculous in the composition of monarchy; it first excludes a man from the means of information, yet empowers him to act in cases where the highest judgment is required. The state of a king shuts him from the world, yet the business of a king requires him to know it thoroughly; wherefore the different parts, unnaturally opposing and destroying each other, prove the whole character to be absurd and useless.

OCTOBER 2

It requires but a very small glance of thought to perceive, that altho' laws made in one generation often continue in force through succeeding generations, yet that they continue to derive their force from the consent of the living. A law not repealed continues in force, not because it *cannot* be repealed, but because it *is not* repealed; and the non-repealing passes for consent.

OCTOBER 3

The God in whom we believe is a God of moral truth, and not a God of mystery or obscurity. Mystery is the antagonist of truth. It is a fog of human invention, that obscures truth and represents it in distortion. Truth never invelops *itself* in mystery; and the mystery in which it is at any time inveloped, is the work of its antagonist, and never of itself.

OCTOBER 4

"REFLECTIONS ON TITLES" (1775)

When I reflect on the pompous titles bestowed on unworthy men, I feel an indignity that instructs me to despise the absurdity.

OCTOBER 5

RIGHTS OF MAN: PART THE SECOND (1792)

Civil government does not consist in executions; but in making that provision for the instruction of youth, and the support of age, as to exclude, as much as possible, profligacy from the one, and despair from the other. Instead of this, the resources of a country are lavished upon kings, upon courts, upon hirelings, imposters, and prostitutes; and even the poor themselves, with all their wants upon them, are compelled to support the fraud that oppresses them.

OCTOBER 6

THE AMERICAN CRISIS, NUMBER I (1776)

Not all the treasures of the world, so far as I believe, could have induced me to support an offensive war; for I think it murder: but if a thief break into my house—burn and destroy my property, and kill, or threaten to kill me and those that are in it, and to "bind me in all cases whatsoever," to his absolute will, am I to suffer it?

OCTOBER 7

WORSHIP AND CHURCH BELLS:
A LETTER TO CAMILLE JORDAN (1797)

The first object for inquiry in all cases, more especially in matters of religious concern, is TRUTH. We ought to inquire into the truth of whatever we are taught to believe, and it is certain that the books called the Scriptures stand in this respect in more than a doubtful predicament.

OCTOBER 8

Hunger is not among the postponeable wants, and a day, even a few hours, in such a condition, is often the crisis of a life of ruin.

OCTOBER 9

What were formerly called Revolutions, were little more than a change of persons, or an alteration of local circumstances. They rose and fell like things of course, and had nothing in their existence or their fate that could influence beyond the spot that produced them. But what we now see in the world, from the Revolutions of America and France, are a renovation of the natural order of things, a system of principles as universal as truth and the existence of man, and combining moral with political happiness and national prosperity.

OCTOBER 10

Small islands not capable of protecting themselves, are the proper objects for kingdoms to take under their care; but there is something very absurd, in supposing a continent to be perpetually governed by an island. In no instance hath nature made the satellite larger than its primary planet, and as England and America, with respect to each other, reverses the common order of nature, it is evident they belong to different systems: England to Europe, America to itself.

OCTOBER 11

PROSPECT PAPERS (1804)

As priestcraft was always the enemy of knowledge, because priestcraft supports itself by keeping people in delusion and ignorance, it was consistent with its policy to make the acquisition of knowledge a real sin.

OCTOBER 12

RIGHTS OF MAN: PART THE SECOND (1792)

In all other cases, a person is a minor until the age of twenty-one years. Before this period, he is not trusted with the management of an acre of land, or with the heritable property of a flock of sheep, or an herd of swine; but, wonderful to tell! he may, at the age of eighteen years, be trusted with a nation.

OCTOBER 13

CASE OF THE OFFICERS OF EXCISE (1772)

The rich, in ease and affluence, may think I have drawn an unnatural portrait; but could they descend to the cold regions of want, the circle of polar poverty, they would find their opinions changing with the climate.

OCTOBER 14

DISSERTATION ON FIRST PRINCIPLES OF GOVERNMENT (1795)

As to that *hospital of incurables* (as Chesterfield calls it) the British House of Peers, it is an excrescence growing out of corruption; and there is no more affinity or resemblance between any of the branches of a legislative body originating from the rights of the people, and the aforesaid house of peers, than between a regular member of the human body and an ulcerated wen.

OCTOBER 15

COMMON SENSE (1776)

The more men have to lose, the less willing are they to venture. The rich are in general slaves to fear, and submit to courtly power with the trembling duplicity of a spaniel.

OCTOBER 16

RIGHTS OF MAN: PART THE FIRST (1791)

What is government more than the management of the affairs of a Nation? It is not, and from its nature cannot be, the property of any particular man or family, but of the whole community, at whose expence it is supported; and though by force or contrivance it has been usurped into an inheritance, the usurpation cannot alter the right of things.

OCTOBER 17

RIGHTS OF MAN: PART THE SECOND (1792)

It requires some talents to be a common mechanic; but, to be a king, requires only the animal figure of man—a sort of breathing automaton.

OCTOBER 18

THE AGE OF REASON: PART THE FIRST (1794)

As the christian system of faith has made a revolution in theology, so also has it made a revolution in the state of learning. That which is now called learning was not learning originally. Learning does not consist, as the schools now make it to consist, in the knowledge of languages, but in the knowledge of things to which language gives names.

OCTOBER 19

RIGHTS OF MAN: PART THE SECOND (1792)

Though the ancient governments present to us a miserable picture of the condition of man, there is one which above all others exempts itself from the general description. I mean the democracy of the Athenians. We see more to admire, and less to condemn, in that great, extraordinary people, than in any thing which history affords.

OCTOBER 20

RIGHTS OF MAN: PART THE FIRST (1791)

The revolutions of America and France have thrown a beam of light over the world.

OCTOBER 21

AGRARIAN JUSTICE (1797)

When the riches of one man above another shall increase the national fund in the same proportion;

when it shall be seen that the prosperity of that fund depends on the prosperity of individuals; when the more riches a man acquires, the better it shall be for the general mass; it is then that antipathies will cease, and property be placed on the permanent basis of national interest and protection.

OCTOBER 22

LETTER ADDRESSED TO THE ADDRESSERS,
ON THE LATE PROCLAMATION (1792)

The Representatives in England appear now to act as if they were afraid to do right, even in part, lest it should awaken the nation to a sense of all the wrongs it has endured.

OCTOBER 23

RIGHTS OF MAN: PART THE FIRST (1791)

Titles are like circles drawn by the magician's wand, to contract the sphere of man's felicity. He lives immured within the Bastille of a word, and surveys at a distance the envied life of man.

OCTOBER 24

All the great laws of society are laws of nature. Those of trade and commerce, whether with respect to the intercourse of individuals, or of nations, are laws of mutual and reciprocal interest. They are followed and obeyed, because it is the interest of the parties so to do, and not on account of any formal laws their governments may impose or interpose.

OCTOBER 25

If I do not believe as you believe, it proves that you do not believe as I believe, and this is all that it proves.

OCTOBER 26

It matters very little now, what the King of England either says or does; he hath wickedly broken through every moral and human obligation, trampled nature and conscience beneath his feet; and by a steady and constitutional spirit of insolence and cruelty, procured for himself an universal hatred.

OCTOBER 27

THE AGE OF REASON: PART THE FIRST (1794)

When also I am told that a woman, called the Virgin Mary, said, or gave out, that she was with child without any cohabitation with a man, and that her betrothed husband, Joseph, said, that an angel told him so, I have a right to believe them or not: such a circumstance required a much stronger evidence than their bare word for it: but we have not even this; for neither Joseph nor Mary wrote any such matter themselves. It is only reported by others that *they said so*. It is hearsay upon hearsay, and I do not chuse to rest my belief upon such evidence.

OCTOBER 28

RIGHTS OF MAN: PART THE SECOND (1792)

It is time that nations should be rational, and not be governed like animals, for the pleasure of their riders.

OCTOBER 29

COMMON SENSE (1776)

Here then is the origin and rise of government; namely, a mode rendered necessary by the inability of moral virtue to govern the world; here too is the design and end of government, viz. freedom and security.

OCTOBER 30

RIGHTS OF MAN: PART THE FIRST (1791)

On this question of war, three things are to be considered. First, the right of declaring it: Secondly, the expence of supporting it: Thirdly, the mode of conducting it after it is declared. The French constitution places the *right* where the *expence* must fall, and this union can be only in the nation. The mode of conducting it after it is declared, it consigns to the executive department.—Were this the case in all countries, we should hear but little more of wars.

OCTOBER 31

COMMON SENSE (1776)

It is not in numbers but in unity, that our great strength lies.

NOVEMBER

Independence was a doctrine scarce and rare even towards the conclusion of the year Seventy-five: All our politics had been founded on the hope or expectation of making the matter up—a hope, which, though general on the side of America, had never entered the head or heart of the British court. Their hope was conquest and confiscation. Good Heavens! what volumes of thanks does America owe to Britain! What infinite obligations to the fool, that fills, with paradoxical vacancy, the throne! Nothing but the sharpest essence of villany, compounded with the strongest distillation of folly, could have produced a menstruum that would have effected a separation.

The American Crisis, Number III (1777)

NOVEMBER 1

RIGHTS OF MAN: PART THE FIRST (1791)

In reviewing the history of the English Government, its wars and its taxes, a by-stander, not blinded by prejudice, nor warped by interest, would declare, that taxes were not raised to carry on wars, but that wars were raised to carry on taxes.

NOVEMBER 2

THE AGE OF REASON: PART THE SECOND (1795)

Whence arose all the horrid assassination of whole nations of men, women, and infants, with which the bible is filled, and the bloody persecutions and tortures unto death, and religious wars, that since that time, have laid Europe in blood and ashes? Whence arose they, but from this impious thing called revealed religion: and this monstrous belief that God had spoken to man.

NOVEMBER 3

REASONS FOR PRESERVING THE LIFE OF LOUIS CAPET (1793)

As far as my experience in public life extends, I have ever observed, that the great mass of the people are invariably just, both in their intentions and in their objects; but the true method of accomplishing an effect does not always show itself in the first instance.

NOVEMBER 4

"TO HENRY LAURENS" (1778?)

The first useful class of citizens are the farmers and cultivators. These may be called citizens of the first necessity, because every thing comes originally from the earth. . . .

Perhaps you will say that in this classification of citizens I have marked no place for myself; that I am neither farmer, mechanic, merchant nor shopkeeper. I believe, however, I am of the first class. I am a *farmer of thoughts*, and all the crops I raise I give away. I please myself with making you a present of the thoughts in this letter.

NOVEMBER 5

WORSHIP AND CHURCH BELLS: A LETTER TO CAMILLE JORDAN (1797)

One good schoolmaster is of more use than a hundred priests.

NOVEMBER 6

THE FORESTER'S LETTERS (1776)

To live beneath the authority of those whom we cannot love, is misery, slavery, or what name you please.

NOVEMBER 7

DISSERTATION ON FIRST PRINCIPLES OF GOVERNMENT (1795)

Nothing can present to our judgment, or to our imagination, a figure of greater absurdity than that of seeing the government of a nation fall, as it frequently does into the hands of a lad necessarily destitute of experience, and often little better than a fool. It is an insult to every man of years, of character, and of talent, in a country.

NOVEMBER 8

"THE CRISIS, NUMBER VIII" (1780)

Such excesses of passionate folly, and unjust as well as unwise resentment, have driven you on, like Pharoah, to unpitied miseries, and while the importance of that quarrel shall perpetuate your disgrace, the flag of America will carry it round the world. The natural feelings of every rational being will take against you, and wherever the story shall be told, you will have neither excuse nor consolation left. With an unsparing hand and an unsatiable mind, you have havocked the world, both to gain dominion and to lose it, and while, in a frenzy of avarice and ambition, the east and west were doomed to tributary bondage, you rapidly earned destruction as the wages of a nation.

NOVEMBER 9

RIGHTS OF MAN: PART THE SECOND (1792)

It is to the great and fundamental principles of society and civilization—to the common usage universally consented to, and mutually and reciprocally maintained—to the unceasing circulation of interest, which, passing through its million channels, invigorates the whole mass of civilized man—it is to these things, infinitely more than to any thing which even the best instituted government can perform, that the safety and prosperity of the individual and of the whole depends.

NOVEMBER 10

COMMON SENSE (1776)

Is the power who is jealous of our prosperity, a proper power to govern us? Whoever says *No* to this question is an *independant*, for independancy means no more, than, whether we shall make our own laws, or, whether the king, the greatest enemy this continent hath, or can have, shall tell us "*there shall be no laws but such as I like.*"

NOVEMBER 11

RIGHTS OF MAN: PART THE FIRST (1791)

The frivolous matters upon which war is made, shew the disposition and avidity of Governments to uphold the system of war, and betray the motives upon which they act.

NOVEMBER 12

CONSTITUTIONS, GOVERNMENTS, AND CHARTERS (1805)

A constitution is the act of the people in their original character of sovereignty. A government is a creature of the constitution; it is produced and brought into existence by it. A constitution defines and limits the powers of the government it creates. It therefore follows, as a natural and also a logical result, that the governmental exercise of any power not authorized by the constitution is an assumed power, and therefore illegal.

NOVEMBER 13

THE AMERICAN CRISIS, NUMBER III (1777)

That men never turn rogues without turning fools, is a maxim, sooner or later, universally true.

NOVEMBER 14

PROSPECTS ON THE RUBICON (1787)

That jealousy which individuals of every nation feel at the supposed design of foreign powers, fits them to be the prey of ministers, and of those among themselves whose trade is war.

NOVEMBER 15

"TO SAMUEL ADAMS" (1803)

I endangered my own life, in the first place, by opposing in the Convention the execution of the King, and by laboring to show they were trying the monarchy and not the man, and that the crimes imputed to him were the crimes of the monarchical system; and I endangered it a second time by opposing atheism; and yet *some* of your priests, for I do not believe that all are perverse, cry out, in the war-whoop of monarchical priest-craft, What an infidel, what a wicked man, is Thomas Paine! They might as well add, for he believes in God and is against shedding blood.

NOVEMBER 16

COMMON SENSE (1776)

Absolute governments (tho' the disgrace of human nature) have this advantage with them, that they are simple; if the people suffer, they know the head from which their suffering springs, know likewise the remedy, and are not bewildered by a variety of causes and cures.

NOVEMBER 17

"THE CRISIS, NUMBER XI" (1782)

We sometimes experience sensations to which language is not equal. The conception is too bulky to be born alive, and in the torture of thinking we stand dumb. Our feelings imprisoned by their magnitude, find no way out, and, in the struggle of expression, every finger tries to be a tongue. The machinery of the body seems too little for the mind and we look about for helps to shew our thoughts by.

NOVEMBER 18

RIGHTS OF MAN: PART THE SECOND (1792)

Every aristocratical family has an appendage of family beggars hanging round it, which in a few ages, or a few generations, are shook off, and console themselves with telling their tale in alms-houses, workhouses, and prisons. This is the natural consequence of aristocracy.

NOVEMBER 19

"EXAMINATION OF THE PROPHECIES" (1802)

The prejudice of unfounded belief, often degenerates into the prejudice of custom, and becomes at last rank hypocrisy.

NOVEMBER 20

RIGHTS OF MAN: PART THE SECOND (1792)

To inherit a government, is to inherit the people, as if they were flocks and herds.

NOVEMBER 21

RIGHTS OF MAN: PART THE FIRST (1791)

With what ideas of justice or honour can that man enter a house of legislation, who absorbs in his own person the inheritance of a whole family of children, or doles out to them some pitiful portion with the insolence of a gift?

NOVEMBER 22

COMMON SENSE (1776)

These proceedings may at first appear strange and difficult; but, like all other steps which we have already passed over, will in a little time become familiar and agreeable; and, until an independance is declared, the Continent will feel itself like a man who continues putting off some unpleasant business from day to day, yet knows it must be done, hates to set about it, wishes it over, and is continually haunted with the thoughts of its necessity.

NOVEMBER 23

AGRARIAN JUSTICE (1797)

The rugged face of society, chequered with the extremes of affluence and of want, proves that some extraordinary violence has been committed upon it, and calls on justice for redress. The great mass of the poor, in all countries, are become an hereditary race, and it is next to impossible for them to get out of that state of themselves. It ought also to be observed, that this mass increases in all countries that are called civilized.

NOVEMBER 24

THE AMERICAN CRISIS, NUMBER II (1777)

It is surprising to what pitch of infatuation blind folly and obstinacy will carry mankind.

NOVEMBER 25

PROSPECT PAPERS (1804)

It is to be hoped some humane person will, on account of our people on the frontiers, as well as of the Indians, undeceive them with respect to the present the missionaries have made them, and which they call a *good book*, containing, they say, *the will and laws of the* GREAT SPIRIT. Can those missionaries suppose that the assassination of men, women and children, and sucking infants, related in the books ascribed to Moses, Joshua, etc., and blasphemously said to be done by the command of the Lord, the Great Spirit, can be edifying to our Indian neighbors, or advantageous to us?

NOVEMBER 26

RIGHTS OF MAN: PART THE SECOND (1792)

It is for the good of nations, and not for the emolument or aggrandizement of particular individuals, that government ought to be established, and that mankind are at the expence of supporting it.

NOVEMBER 27

THE FORESTER'S LETTERS (1776)

Nature seems sometimes to laugh at mankind, by giving them so many fools for kings; at other times, she punishes their folly by giving them tyrants; but England must have offended highly to be cursed with both in one.

NOVEMBER 28

COMMON SENSE (1776)

In America THE LAW IS KING.

NOVEMBER 29

RIGHTS OF MAN: PART THE SECOND (1792)

It can only be by blinding the understanding of man, and making him believe that government is some wonderful mysterious thing, that exessive revenues are obtained. Monarchy is well calculated to ensure this end. It is the property of government; a thing kept up to amuse the ignorant, and quiet them into taxes.

NOVEMBER 30

"TO SAMUEL ADAMS" (1803)

Our relation to each other in this world is as men, and the man who is a friend to man and to his rights, let his religious opinions be what they may, is a good citizen, to whom I can give, as I ought to do, and as every other ought, the right hand of fellowship, and to none with more hearty good will, my dear friend, than to you.

DECEMBER

Putting then aside, as matter of distinct consideration, the outrage offered to the moral justice of God, by supposing him to make the innocent suffer for the guilty, and also the loose morality and low contrivance of supposing him to change himself into the shape of a man, in order to make an excuse to himself for not executing his supposed sentence upon Adam; putting, I say, those things aside, as matter of distinct consideration, it is certain, that what is called the christian system of faith, including in it the whimsical account of the creation; the strange story of Eve, the snake, and the apple; the amphibious idea of a man-god; the corporeal idea of the death of a god; the mythological idea of a family of gods, and the christian system of arithmetic, that three are one, and one is three, are all irreconcilable, not only to the divine gift of reason that God has given to man, but to the knowledge that man gains of the power and wisdom of God, by the aid of the sciences, and by studying the structure of the universe that God has made.

The Age of Reason: Part the First (1794)

୧ଓ ଲ୨

DECEMBER 1

RIGHTS OF MAN: PART THE SECOND (1792)

When, in countries that are called civilized, we see age going to the workhouse and youth to the gallows, something must be wrong in the system of government.

DECEMBER 2

THE AMERICAN CRISIS, NUMBER III (1777)

We have crouded the business of an age into the compass of a few months, and have been driven through such a rapid succession of things, that, for the want of leisure to think, we unavoidably wasted knowledge as we came, and have left nearly as much behind us as we brought with us: But the road is yet rich with the fragments, and, before we fully lose sight of them, will repay us for the trouble of stopping to pick them up.

DECEMBER 3

RIGHTS OF MAN: PART THE FIRST (1791)

All the children which the aristocracy disowns (which are all, except the eldest) are, in general, cast like orphans on a parish, to be provided for by the public, but at a greater charge.—Unnecessary offices and places in governments and courts are created at the expence of the public, to maintain them.

DECEMBER 4

THE AGE OF REASON: PART THE SECOND (1795)

Of all the systems of religion that ever were invented, there is none more derogatory to the Almighty, more unedifying to man, more repugnant to reason, and more contradictory in itself than this thing called Christianity. Too absurd for belief, too impossible to convince, and too inconsistent for practice, it renders the heart torpid, or produces only atheists and fanatics. As an engine of power it serves the purpose of despotism; and as a means of wealth, the avarice of priests; but so far as respects the good of man in general, it leads to nothing here or hereafter.

DECEMBER 5

THE FORESTER'S LETTERS (1776)

A republican form of government is pointed out by nature—kingly governments by an unequality of power. In republican governments, the leaders of the people, if improper, are removable by vote; kings only by arms: an unsuccessful vote in the first case, leaves the voter safe; but an unsuccessful attempt in the latter, is death. Strange, that that which is our *right* in the *one*, should be our *ruin* in the *other*.

DECEMBER 6

COMMON SENSE (1776)

Government, like dress, is the badge of lost innocence; the palaces of kings are built on the ruins of the bowers of paradise.

DECEMBER 7

RIGHTS OF MAN: PART THE SECOND (1792)

The defects of every government and constitution, both as to principle and form must, on a parity of reasoning, be as open to discussion as the defects of a law, and it is a duty which every man owes to society to point them out. When those defects, and the means of remedying them are generally seen by a nation, that nation will reform its government or its constitution in the one case, as the government repealed or reformed the law in the other.

DECEMBER 8

Thus necessity, like a gravitating power, would soon form our newly arrived emigrants into society, the reciprocal blessings of which, would supercede, and render the obligations of law and government unnecessary while they remained perfectly just to each other; but as nothing but heaven is impregnable to vice, it will unavoidably happen, that in proportion as they surmount the first difficulties of emigration, which bound them together in a common cause, they will begin to relax in their duty and attachment to each other; and this remissness, will point out the necessity, of establishing some form of government to supply the defect of moral virtue.

DECEMBER 9

Can any thing be more limited, and at the same time more capricious, than the qualifications of electors are in England? Limited—because not one man in an hundred (I speak much within compass) is admitted to vote: Capricious—because the lowest character that can be supposed to exist, and who has not so much as the visible means of an honest livelihood, is an elector in some places; while, in other places, the man who pays very large taxes, and has a known fair character, and the farmer who rents to the amount of three or four hundred pounds a year, with a property on that farm to three or four times that amount, is not admitted to be an elector.

DECEMBER 10
"EPISTLE TO QUAKERS" (1776)

And here, without anger or resentment, I bid you farewell. Sincerely wishing, that as men and Christians, ye may always fully and uninterruptedly enjoy every civil and religious right, and be, in your turn, the means of securing it to others; but that the example which ye have unwisely set, of mingling religion with politics, *may be disavowed and reprobated by every inhabitant of* AMERICA.

DECEMBER 11
RIGHTS OF MAN: PART THE SECOND (1792)

The aristocracy are not the farmers who work the land, and raise the produce, but are the mere consumers of the rent; and when compared with the active world, are the drones, a seraglio of males, who neither collect the honey nor form the hive, but exist only for lazy enjoyment.

DECEMBER 12

Every national church or religion has established itself by pretending some special mission from God communicated to certain individuals. The Jews have their Moses; the Christians their Jesus Christ, their apostles and saints; and the Turks their Mahomet; as if the way to God was not open to every man alike.

Each of those churches show certain books which they call *revelation*, or the word of God. The Jews say that their word of God was given by God to Moses face to face; the Christians say, that their word of God came by divine inspiration; and the Turks say, that their word of God (the Koran) was brought by an angel from heaven. Each of those churches accuses the other of unbelief; and, for my own part, I disbelieve them all.

DECEMBER 13

The landholder, the farmer, the manufacturer, the merchant, the tradesman, and every occupation, prospers by the aid which each receives from the other, and from the whole. Common interest regulates their concerns, and forms their law; and the laws which common usage ordains, have a greater influence than the laws of government. In fine, soci-

ety performs for itself almost every thing which is
ascribed to government.

DECEMBER 14

RIGHTS OF MAN: PART THE FIRST (1791)

The despotism of Louis XIV, united with the gaiety of
his Court, and the gaudy ostentation of his character,
had so humbled, and at the same time so fascinated
the mind of France, that the people appeared to have
lost all sense of their own dignity, in contemplating
that of their Grand Monarch.

DECEMBER 15

RIGHTS OF MAN: PART THE SECOND (1792)

Excess and inequality of taxation, however disguised
in the means, never fail to appear in their effects. As
a great mass of the community are thrown thereby
into poverty and discontent, they are constantly
on the brink of commotion; and, deprived, as they
unfortunately are, of the means of information,
are easily heated to outrage. Whatever the appar-
ent cause of any riots may be, the real one is always
want of happiness. It shews that something is wrong
in the system of government, that injures the felicity
by which society is to be preserved.

DECEMBER 16

WHEREFORE, instead of gazing at each other with suspicious or doubtful curiosity, let each of us, hold out to his neighbour the hearty hand of friendship, and unite in drawing a line, which, like an act of oblivion, shall bury in forgetfulness every former dissention. Let the names of Whig and Tory be extinct; and let none other be heard among us, than those of *a good citizen, an open and resolute friend, and a virtuous supporter of the* RIGHTS *of* MANKIND *and of the* FREE AND INDEPENDANT STATES OF AMERICA.

DECEMBER 17

Man has no authority over posterity in matters of personal right; and therefore, no man, or body of men, had, or can have, a right to set up hereditary government.

DECEMBER 18

I am thus far a Quaker, that I would gladly agree with all the world to lay aside the use of arms, and settle matters by negotiation; but unless the whole will, the matter ends, and I take up my musket and thank heaven he has put it in my power.

DECEMBER 19

RIGHTS OF MAN: PART THE SECOND (1792)

Would we make any office hereditary that required wisdom and abilities to fill it? and where wisdom and abilities are not necessary, such an office, whatever it may be, is superfluous or insignificant.

DECEMBER 20

"THE CRISIS, NUMBER VIII" (1780)

Hitherto you have experienced the expences, but nothing of the miseries of war. Your disappointments have been accompanied with no immediate suffering, and your losses came to you only by intelligence. Like fire at a distance, you heard not even the cry; you felt not the danger, you saw not the confusion. To you every thing has been foreign but the taxes to support it. You knew not what it was to be alarmed at midnight with an armed enemy in the streets. You were strangers to the distressing scene of a family in flight, and to the thousand restless cares and tender sorrows that incessantly arose.

DECEMBER 21

RIGHTS OF MAN: PART THE FIRST (1791)

What are the present Governments of Europe, but a scene of iniquity and oppression? What is that of England? Do not its own inhabitants say, It is a market where every man has his price, and where corruption is common traffic, at the expence of a deluded people?

DECEMBER 22

THE AMERICAN CRISIS, NUMBER I (1776)

I have as little superstition in me as any man living: but my secret opinion has ever been, and still is, that God will not give up a people to military destruction, or leave them unsupportedly to perish, who had so earnestly and so repeatedly fought to avoid the calamities of war, by every decent method which wisdom could invent. Neither have I so much of the infidel in me, as to suppose that he has relinquished the government of the world, and given us up to the care of devils: and as I do not, I cannot see on what grounds the king can look up to heaven for help against us. A common murderer, a highwayman, or a housebreaker, has as good a pretence as he.

DECEMBER 23

It is the nature and intention of a constitution to *prevent governing by party*, by establishing a common principle that shall limit and controul the power and impulse of party, and that says to all parties, THUS FAR SHALT THOU GO, AND NO FARTHER. But in the absence of a constitution, men look entirely to party, and instead of principle governing party, party governs principle.

DECEMBER 24

The past treatment of Africans must naturally fill them with abhorrence of Christians; lead them to think our religion would make them more inhuman savages, if they embraced it; thus the gain of that trade has been pursued in opposition to the Redeemer's cause, and the happiness of men. Are we not, therefore, bound in duty to him and to them to repair these injuries, as far as possible, by taking some proper measures to instruct, not only the slaves here, but the Africans in their own countries? Primitive Christians labored always to spread their *divine religion*; and this is equally our duty while there is an heathen nation. But what singular obligations are we under to these injured people!

DECEMBER 25

COMMON SENSE (1776)

When we are planning for posterity, we ought to remember that virtue is not hereditary.

DECEMBER 26

RIGHTS OF MAN: PART THE FIRST (1791)

That which may be thought right and found convenient in one age, may be thought wrong and found inconvenient in another. In such cases, Who is to decide, the living, or the dead?

DECEMBER 27

"ON THE AFFAIRS OF PENNSYLVANIA" (1786)

The Plough and the Sail are the Arms of the state of Pennsylvania, and their connection should be held in remembrance by all good citizens.

DECEMBER 28

"COMMON SENSE, ON FINANCING THE WAR" (1782)

The union of America is the foundation-stone of

her independence; the rock on which it is built; and is something so sacred in her constitution, that we ought to watch every word we speak, and every thought we think, that we injure it not, even by mistake.

DECEMBER 29
THE AMERICAN CRISIS, NUMBER III (1777)

In the progress of politics, as in the common occurrences of life, we are not only apt to forget the ground we have travelled over, but frequently neglect to gather up experience as we go.

DECEMBER 30
THE AMERICAN CRISIS, NUMBER II (1777)

This Continent, Sir, is too extensive to sleep all at once, and too watchful, even in its slumbers, not to startle at the unhallowed foot of an invader.

DECEMBER 31
COMMON SENSE (1776)

We have it in our power to begin the world over again.

Editor Bio

Edward G. Gray is professor of history at Florida State University and author of *Tom Paine's Iron Bridge: Building a United States*. He is coeditor of the University of Chicago Press series American Beginnings, 1500–1900.

Acknowledgments

I am indebted to two Florida State University graduate students for help with this volume. Alexander Rowney transcribed the quotes, and Amy Coale prepared the index of sources.

Index of Sources

A Note on Sources: No comprehensive scholarly edition of Paine's writings has ever been published. Identifying definitive texts on which such an edition could be based is impossible. Most of the original manuscripts for Paine's published writings have been lost, and the earliest printed versions often show slight variation from one edition to the next. In an effort to identify the most recent and reliable texts, this volume draws on three editions of Paine's writings. For most of Paine's shorter writings, it uses *The Complete Writings of Thomas Paine*, ed. Philip S. Foner, 2 vols. (New York: Citadel Press, 1945). For Paine's longer political writings, it uses the more up-to-date *"Rights of Man," "Common Sense," and Other Political Writings*, ed. Mark Philp (Oxford: Oxford University Press, 1995). For *The Age of Reason*, the *American Crisis* essays, and several shorter newspaper pieces identified after the publication of *The Complete Writings*, it draws on *Thomas Paine: Collected Writings*, ed. Eric Foner (New York: Library of America, 1995).

Constitutions, Governments, and Charters, November 12

"The Crisis, Number VI," May 4, August 3

"The Crisis, Number VII," March 4, July (general)

"The Crisis, Number VIII," February 8, April 10, July 25, September 22, October (general), November 8, December 20

"The Crisis, Number IX," September 29

"The Crisis, Number XI," January 15, January 23, November 17

Dissertation on First Principles of Government, January 27, February 16, May 14, June 4, July 11, July 29, August 10, August 20, September 14, October 14, November 7, December 23

Dissertations on Government, March 2, April 2, May 6, July 3, September 24

"The Dream Interpreted," March 8

"Emancipation of Slaves," July 21

"Epistle to Quakers," December 10

"An Essay for the Use of New Republicans in Their Opposition to Monarchy," March 21

"An Essay on Dream," January 31, August 26

"Examination of the Prophecies," September 11, November 19

The Forester's Letters, January 22, February 21, May 9, June 13, July 23, November 6, November 27, December 5

"Forgetfulness," February 11

"The Last Crisis, Number XIII," March 7, June 15, July 10, July 15, September 13

Letter Addressed to the Addressers, on the Late Proclamation, January 3, February 17, March (general), March 10, March 17, May 18, May 22, June 20, August 6, September 9, September 16, October 22

Letter to the Abbé Raynal, January 8, February 13, February 23, April 7, April 26, June 28, July 22, September 30

12, September 17, September 21, September 26, October
5, October 8, October 12, October 17, October 19, October
24, October 28, November 9, November 18, November 20,
November 26, November 29, December 1, December 7,
December 11, December 13, December 15, December 17,
December 19

"Shall Louis XVI Be Respited?," January 21
Six Letters to Rhode Island, January 4

"Thoughts on Defensive War," December 18
To Benjamin Rush, June 19
To Danton, February 5, June 22, July 24, August 12, September
    6
"To Henry Laurens," November 4
"To Samuel Adams," February 4, March 29, August 29, Octo-
    ber 25, November 15, November 30
"To the Authors of *The Republican*," January 12, May 8
To the Citizens of the United States, January 5, January 28,
    August 15, August 22
"To the Earl of Shelburne," April 27, August 28

Worship and Church Bells: A Letter to Camille Jordan, May 3,
    May 11, August 16, October 7, November 5